Room to Grow

A STUDY OF THE BOOK OF PHILIPPIANS

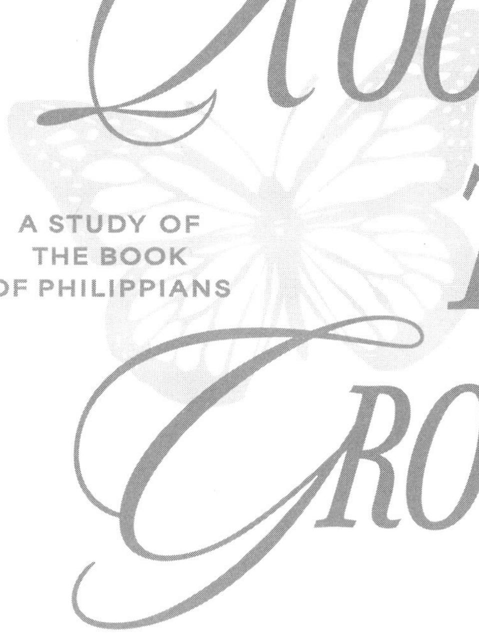

Book design by Faith Hyman
Theological Editing by Aubrey Johnston
Editing by Madison Perry

Delight Ministries
www.delightministries.com

Printed in the United States of America
First Printing: January 2026
Color House Graphics
ISBN: 979-8-9988479-1-2

delight

Our Mission

Our mission is to invite college women into **Christ-centered community** that **fosters vulnerability** and **transforms stories.**

Christ-Centered Community

We launch, grow, and **sustain thriving Christ-centered communities** on college campuses. We've seen time and time again that community is often the catalyst for **true Kingdom impact.**

Foster Vulnerability

We aim to provide a **space on college campuses** for women to vulnerably share how Christ has been at work in their lives. We believe that vulnerability leads to **breakthrough, and breakthrough leads to transformation!**

Transform Stories

We believe that **one moment with Jesus can truly change everything.** Our mission is to give college women numerous opportunities to meet with Jesus and **have their lives transformed!**

TABLE OF CONTENTS

HOW TO READ THIS BOOK

Scripture

In this study, we'll be walking through the book of Philippians verse by verse. Each week, you'll be reading a few verses from Paul's letter to the church at Philippi as we work our way through the book. The chapters in this study will guide you through the reading process. As you read, you'll answer questions, fill in the blanks, and hopefully get a deeper understanding of the context behind what you're reading. You'll want to pull out your Bible and start reading anytime you see something like this below:

Read Philippians 4:6-7.

Just remember that this is your cue to pause and open the Word. Please don't skip reading the actual Word of God! We promise that our words pale in comparison to what God can say to you directly through Scripture!

Primarily, we will use the NIV translation when citing Scripture throughout this study. Feel free to use whatever translation works for you, but you might be a tad confused on some of the fill-in-the-blanks if you use a different Bible translation. You can always head to BibleGateway.com to access a free version of the NIV if you need it. Each week, we will zero in on a topic that the Scripture introduces, using three main points to guide our journey through the text. Our prayer is that this book brings new light to Bible lessons and verses that you've perhaps read a million times.

Think it Through

You'll notice that all throughout the book, we ask you questions under the title "Think it Through." These questions are your opportunity to take it deeper, to do some personal reflection, and allow the Scripture to begin to soak into your heart and life. These are moments of evaluating where you're at and embracing the hard truth. Don't just answer how you think you should answer; answer as honestly as possible! There is such freedom to be found when we come before the Lord with all of our mess and imperfections! We promise that as you get vulnerable before the Lord, He will unlock even deeper intimacy.

Conversation Starters

Our goal is to get the conversation rolling between you and the Lord, within your Delight community, or through a small group! These questions found at the end of every chapter will help you do just that. We suggest setting some time aside each week to think through your answers to these questions in a prayerful way with the Lord. Then, come ready to discuss them with whoever you're processing this study with. We promise that the more time you take to prepare on the front end, the better your conversations will be!

Take Your Time

Remember that you have an entire week to get through each chapter! Don't feel like you have to do it all in one sitting. Take your time with it and try to process and understand every last verse. There's no pressure to get through an entire chapter in one day. Break up the content however works best for you!

TIPS FOR READING SCRIPTURE

The truth is, reading Scripture isn't always easy! It's a muscle that you have to stretch and grow over time. We've compiled a list of tips from some of our friends that will help you to start to love your daily time in the Word. These are all practical tips that will help you to better hear the voice of God through the Scripture.

#1 Prepare Your Heart

This is SO simple! Every day before you open the Word, ask God to simply prepare your heart, show up, and speak to you. Reading the Bible isn't something we have to do on our own or through our own power. The Word is alive, meaning that God can and will speak to you through it. All you have to do is ask!

#2 Ask Good Questions

This can seriously change the way you encounter the Bible! The best tool we have to understand the Word of God is our ability to ask the right questions. If you've ever read Scripture and not understood something (a.k.a. us every day of our lives), that's an invitation to ask a question. What? When? How? Where? Who? Why? Dig into your questions and seek out answers!

For some of your more historical or practical questions, you can read biblical commentaries, get a study Bible, or talk to someone you trust with more biblical knowledge or Bible study experience. For the other more complex questions, bring them to the feet of Jesus and simply ask. He cares and can provide answers in some of the coolest ways! This isn't your college calculus class where you have to be afraid of looking silly.

There is a loving, caring, and gentle Father on the other end of the line ready to have dialogue with you.

(If this is new to you . . . don't worry! We're going to ask A LOT of questions about the text together in this book.)

#3 Read at Your Own Pace

Take your time with reading Scripture! You have your entire life to read the Bible. If you want to meditate on one verse for an entire week, do it! If you want to read the entire Bible in a month, do that! Go at the pace that feels comfortable to you. Don't be afraid to slow down and dive really deep in certain parts when you feel led to.

#4 Talk About It

Some of the best moments of revelation from Scripture happen by simply talking about the things you've been reading. This isn't a journey you have to travel alone! Be sure to talk about how God is speaking to you through His Word with your roommate, friends, parents, and your Delight community!

#5 Follow the Spirit

When you're reading your Bible, don't be afraid to change course from where you initially started. You may start out reading Genesis but then feel a nudge to reread that Psalm you heard the other day. Don't ignore those nudges! When you open up your heart to hear from the Lord, He may redirect you to another passage of Scripture. And that is absolutely OK. You never know what He might be leading you to.

BEFORE WE BEGIN

A NOTE FROM THE AUTHOR.

Since college, my favorite Bible verse has been Philippians 1:9 . . .

"And this is my prayer: that your love may abound more and more in knowledge and depth of insight . . ."
Philippians 1:9

You see, I've always been pretty hard on myself. I have these astronomical standards for my achievement, my Bible knowledge, my integrity, my spiritual growth . . . you name it, and I've probably tried to be better at it. Because in my mind, I'm not good enough at *any of it.* When I lash out at my husband or my mom, I tell myself it's because I'm not as patient as a "better Christian" would be. When I fail at work or when I bombed a test in college, my first thought is always that a smarter person would have done better—that *I* should have done better. When I'm on day 13 of skipping my morning devotional time, I entertain a constant stream of thoughts telling me that God expects more of me.

In my own sinful and self-isolated thought patterns, there's a huge gap between myself and the girl God expects and intends me to be. I'm disappointed, everyone around me's disappointed, and *surely* God is disappointed, too.

But here's one of the reasons I'm so obsessed with Scripture: The Bible holds a multitude of clear, simple truths that can, in a moment, combat even the most deep-seated lies you're holding onto.

Right there, in the midst of my self-doubt, self-hate, and self-righteous expectations of my own Christlikeness, I read a verse like Philippians 1:9 and my soul is allowed to take a deep breath.

> "... *that your love may abound more and more* ..."

Here, in the Bible I've been using as a standard for moral living, is an invitation to grow, slowly and step by step. Here, Paul—an apostle set apart by God who also still admitted to bearing many failings—prays that the people he shepherds would grow more and more in their love, their knowledge, and their depth of insight.

In the wonderful miracle of God's never-ending grace, we have *room to grow.*

God doesn't expect us to be anyone other than who we are. Instead, He energizes and equips us to walk hand in hand with Him as He tenderly grows us into who He designed us to be. We have never once disappointed Him, as though He were a God who could be surprised by our bad decisions or our lack of insight. Instead, He is *enamored* with us, the precious daughters He created because He desired to love us intimately for eternity.

And it's from that solid certainty of His endless love for us where we start with this study of the book of Philippians.

We're about to spend ten sessions studying the apostle Paul's letter to the church at Philippi verse by verse in search of the answers to our spiritual growth questions. But we're not trying to grow to earn the approval of man or the approval of God! We're hopping onto this road trip for spiritual growth because we can't wait for another adventure side by side with our Creator! We're eager to look more like Jesus not because we hate who we are now, but because the grace of God met us in our mess and told us there's room to grow—that there's more in store for us.

So, wherever you're starting from, there's room for <u>you</u> in this journey.

If you're the girl who hates her mistakes and expects a biblical beatdown every time you trip and fall, this study will open your eyes to the tender heart of a forgiving God.

If you're the girl who wants to read her Bible more or wants to know who to follow on social media, this study will help you search the Word for practical and tangible steps.

If you're the girl ready to make leaps and bounds in her life of faith, this study can help you dig up the stubborn pride and striving locked in your heart.

And, if you're just beginning to open your eyes to what a life with Jesus can look like, this study can hold your hand as you take that first step.

I don't know about you, but I'm ready to grow! I'm so tired of allowing what I think about myself tell me what to think about God. I'm tired of holding myself to standards the Lord didn't set. I'm tired of thinking I'm not enough for a God who's already more than enough for me. **Join me as we bring our burning questions to the feet of Jesus. He's the only one with all the answers!**

XOXO,
Maggie Sawler
Creative Director
Delight Ministries

01

HOW DO I GROW?

How Do I Grow?

PHILIPPIANS 1:1-11

I was on a walk with a friend my junior year of college when the truth finally came spilling out: *I don't think I'm there,* I sputtered out almost incoherently. *I'm not wise or discerning or patient . . . I'm not like Jesus!*

I had this image in my mind of the classic, rock-solid "grandma" in the faith. You know the one! She's the woman revered for her unwavering commitment to the Lord, her unrivaled memorization of Scripture, and her wise advice. She's the woman her grandkids and great grandkids talk about in awe, she's steadfast, holy . . .

As a junior in college, I panicked because I knew I was *none* of those things. What would my grandkids and great-grandkids say about me? I certainly wasn't a pillar of morality or anywhere near the right person to go to for advice. How was I supposed to leave a legacy when I could barely stick to a morning quiet time routine with any sort of regularity?

My friend's answer to my turmoil rocked me to my core. *But you're not a grandma yet,* she said. *You've got time. It's OK that you're not there yet.*

What if God knows you're not who you want to be right now? What if God is completely aware of the gap between your character and His? What if God—perfect in His standards and His holiness—sees you as you are and says, *Daughter, there's room to grow.*

We're about to embark on a ten week study of the book of Philippians, a letter from the Apostle Paul to a church he loved dearly. Paul invites his readers to expand and advance in their love for God and others, in their knowledge of the Word, and in their discernment in order to grow in their faith.

So I think we can extend that invitation to ourselves, too! We're all entering into this study in different phases of our faith walks. Maybe some of you have been walking with the Lord for your whole life and you've found yourself feeling a little stagnant. *Sister, there's more for you!* Maybe you're the girl in Bible study who feels like she doesn't measure up; the other women seem to know more Scripture, act more obedient, pray more confidently. *Friend, it's OK that you aren't there yet!* Or perhaps this is one of the very first times you've cracked open your Bible and you're not even sure if you have a "faith" to begin with. *This Word is for you, too!*

We're all not there yet. We've all got room to grow! And I believe God's words through Paul in the book of the Philippians are an excellent place to start on our journey to becoming wise old grandmas. So let's jump in!

Read Philippians 1:1-11.

OK, let's grab some quick context before we jump into the meaty stuff. The book of Philippians is one of the "Prison Epistles" written by the Apostle Paul while he was, you guessed it, *in prison.* When he penned this letter specifically, Paul was under house arrest in Rome (you can read about it in Acts 28) for his bold preaching of the gospel of Jesus Christ.

Now, Paul is known for being quite the letter writer. In fact, most of what makes up the New Testament of your Bible consists of letters Paul wrote to various churches he was in contact with. This letter was sent to one of his favorites: the church in Philippi. Paul had helped found this community of believers in Philippi some 11 years before writing this letter; the Philippian church in Northern Greece was actually the first place in Europe to hear the good news about Jesus. (You can read about this founding story in Acts 16 if you're interested!)

We can tell these Philippian believers are some of his favorites because of the love and joy evident in every sentence. In fact, Philippians is often referred to as the happiest of Paul's letters! (If you flip through some of the others, you'll see pretty quickly that Paul's not always as mushy gushy as he comes across in this book.)

+ Did you catch onto the "happy" tone when you read Paul's opening prayer in verses 1-11? Which phrases or verses stuck out to you the most?

The intro we read in verses 1-11 is Paul's opening prayer: a greeting and blessing all wrapped up in one. He's thanking God for the believers at Philippi and reaffirming how much he loves them.

And, as we read the beginning of this letter from thousands of years ago that, somehow, has God's power at work in and through it, here's the question we're going to try to answer: *How do I grow?* We've established that we're not quite "there yet" in our faith (wise old grammies we are not!) and we've established that God gives us grace and permission and *room* to grow (He's just that good!) so all that's left is the *how*.

STOP & PRAY

LORD, I PRAISE YOU FOR THE GRACE YOU'VE GIVEN ME TO GROW IN MY FAITH. PLEASE OPEN MY HEART TO YOUR WORD AND SHOW ME HOW TO BECOME A LITTLE BIT MORE LIKE YOU EVERY DAY.

Here's step one in our "how to grow" formula, according to Paul:

01 GROW BY GOD'S POWER

+ FILL IN THE BLANKS FROM PHILIPPIANS 1:6.

"being confident of this, that ______ who ________ a good work in you will __________ it on to __________ until the day __________ of Christ Jesus."

Theologians tend to agree that verse 6 is a sort of motto or "theme" for the entire book of Philippians.[1] Paul is confident that God's the one doing the work (the work being our growth toward unity with Christ and conformity to His mission. Or, if you're really fancy, you can call it *sanctification*). He's confident that God is a good worker who *completes* His work.[2] And, He's confident that God is happy and willing to work in and through broken people (the believers of Philippi and, by extension, us).

I know us perfectionist, hard-worker types are cringing in our seats right now. We're six verses in and Paul's already called out our pride. Sure, we want to grow. But, so often, we want to grow in our own power. We want the credit and the claim to fame! We want to know the secret to the fast track to a shiny, A+ faith so we can pull ourselves up by our boot straps and make it happen. As ugly as it sounds, we secretly want to be able to look down on other believers who aren't as far along as we are because "they haven't worked as hard."

+ On a scale of 1-10, how much do you relate to wanting to grow by your own power?

1 |—|—|—|—|—|—|—|—|—| 10

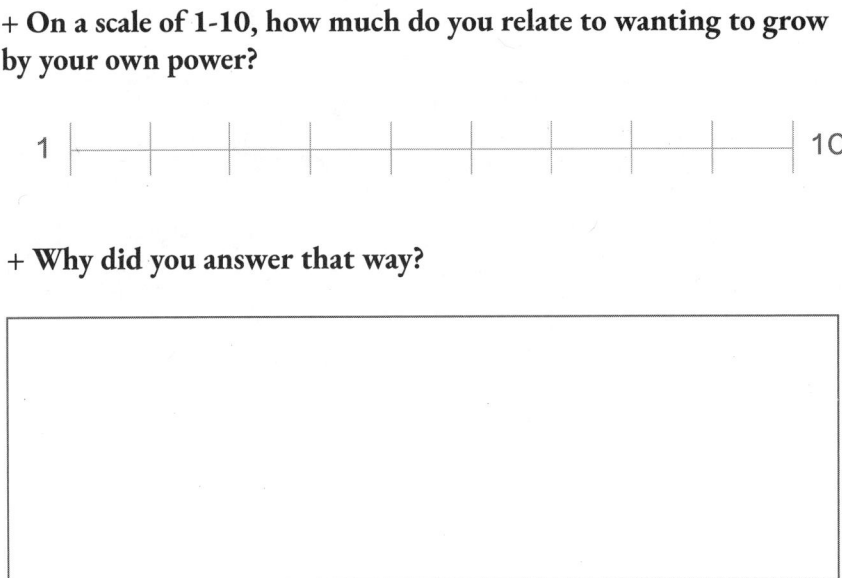

+ Why did you answer that way?

But this is the miracle and the mystery of God's upside-down kingdom: God's the one who does the work. He's the author and finisher of our faith (Hebrews 12:2). He's the one who lights the fire *and* the one who fans the flame. The first step to growing in the Lord is accepting the fact that the Lord is the one who does the growing in us. Our role is to submit, surrender, and join in on the fun!

> *"The important thing throughout is that at every stage of the process–when people first hear the gospel, when they believe it, when they begin to live by it, and when they make progress in faith and love–nothing is done to the glory of the people concerned, as though they were able arrogantly to advance their own cause. Everything is done, as he insists here, 'through King Jesus' and 'to the glory and praise of God.'"*
>
> *N. T. Wright*[3]

Here's the crux of it all. Yes, we're reading a book about how to grow. And yes, we're called to grow in our faith! But *we don't want any growth apart from Jesus.*

+ It's so important that we feel confident in the baseline of God's power before we move on . . . So let's make sure we're all on the same page! In the space below, write it out for yourself: *"I don't want any growth apart from Jesus!"*

Alright, time for step two!

02 GROW IN LOVE

+ FILL IN THE BLANKS FROM PHILIPPIANS 1:9-11.

"And this is my prayer: that your ________ may abound ________ and ________ in knowledge and depth of insight, so that you may be able to discern what is best and may be pure and blameless for the day of Christ, filled with the fruit of righteousness that comes through Jesus Christ—to the glory and praise of God."

If I think too hard about the verse on the last page or meditate on it too long, I always end up crying. Because, get this: I really do *love* Jesus. I loved Him when He spoke to me in third grade and as I began to journal my prayers for the first time. I loved Him in high school when He carried me through a chronic illness and gave me miracles I didn't even know to ask for. I loved Him as He carried me through grief and infertility in my post grad years.

But, as much as I love Him, I am constantly and consistently reminded that *He loves me so much more.* The gap between what my heart can muster up in love and affection for my Creator and His grand, sweeping, larger-than-life love toward me is *huge*. It's almost defeating to realize it: the way I love Him could never compare to how He loves me.

Then, I read a verse like Philippians 1:9 and my world is rocked. *There's room to grow, even in love!* Through His Word, God invites our love to abound more and more. He's drawing us deeper into the mystery of communion with Him. A heart that feels like it could burst now with gratitude and affection and tenderness toward God has the potential to expand in new ways, becoming capable of a love greater than we thought possible at the beginning of our faith journeys.

But, our love for God isn't the only kind of love we're called to grow in. We also need to grow in our love for *each other.*

"Everyone who believes that Jesus is the Christ is born of God, and everyone who loves the father loves his children as well. This is how we know that we love the children of God: by loving God and carrying out his commands."
1 John 5:1–2 (emphasis added)

As Christians, the more we grow in our love for God, the more we will grow in our love for the people around us.[4] It's inevitable! A side effect of passionate love for God is that, bit by bit, we catch onto His heart. We begin to love what He loves, and His children are certainly at the top of the list!

We'll get deeper into this idea of loving the people God has placed in our path as we continue on in this study (it's a biggie for Paul!), so let's leave it here for now: as we pray to grow in our faith, we must pray that God would grow our love not only for Him but also for His people "in knowledge and depth of insight, so that [we] may be able to discern what is best and may be pure and blameless for the day of Christ" (Philippians 1:9b-10).

NOTES:

THINK IT THROUGH

+ What do you love about God? How would you describe your level of love and affection toward Him in this season of your life? (It's OK to get super honest here!)

+ Now, consider how well you love the people around you. Do you see any opportunities for growth in this area?

For step three of our "how-to-grow" strategy, we're going to zoom out a little bit and look at these first 11 verses holistically.

+ Look back at Philippians 1:1-11 in your Bible and underline every time you see the word "pray."

This is the most tangible growth step there is! Do you want to grow? *Girl, you gotta pray!*

03 Grow Through Prayer

It's no accident that Paul began his address to the Philippian believers with a prayer. In verse 3, he shares that he thanks God for them often. Then, in verse 4, he remarks that he prays with joy for them. In verse 7, he reminds them that they are in his heart, and then he actually lists out a specific prayer he's been praying for them in verse 9. It's clear here that Paul's a praying man and that He believes in the power of prayer. Arguably, you might even say that Paul bases a lot of the success of the Philippian church on prayers that have been offered to God on their behalf. Certainly, he would also assume the success of our own spiritual growth would depend on prayer, too, right?

And it should get us thinking . . . *Do we pray like Paul?*

I saw a TikTok video that's been playing on repeat in my mind ever since the day I saw it. A preacher was addressing our often stagnant prayer lives, saying, *If every single thing you prayed for in the past week was answered with a "yes," would the world look any different?*

NOTES:

I was stunned! The only difference my prayers from that week would make is better weather and a shorter line at Starbucks.

How convicting is that?! If I really believed in the power of prayer as Paul seems to, shouldn't my prayers be bigger? Wider-reaching? Less selfish? I want to be the girl who spends solid time contending for my friends who don't know the Lord, asking for miracles for those in crisis, and even asking God to prompt my heart to pray for what He wants me to pray for. But, most of the time, *I'm not.* (Please tell me you can relate!)

+ Find 1 Thessalonians 5:17 and copy it down in the space below.

It's God's will for us to pray. It's such a simple concept but crazy hard to put into action in our busy lives. So instead of sitting in condemnation or frustration about where we're lacking in our call to pray, let's allow this to kick-start baby steps of growth in our prayer journeys!

Sure, you might not be praying without ceasing right now, but you could try praying before every meal.

Sure, you might trip over your words when you get nervous to pray out loud, but you could try praying a Bible verse over a friend who needs it.

Sure, you might not have a burden on your heart to pray for revival yet, but you could start with gratitude.

+ What "baby step" would you like to take in your prayer life?

KEEP GROWING

FEELING STUCK IN YOUR PRAYER JOURNEY? TRY OUT THE ACTS PRAYER FORMAT! BEGIN YOUR PRAYER WITH ADORATION (HONORING AND PRAISING GOD), THEN MOVE ONTO CONFESSION, THANKSGIVING, THEN SUPPLICATION (ASKING GOD FOR THINGS!) THIS SIMPLE FORMAT HELPS ORGANIZE YOUR THOUGHTS AND GIVES YOU A GREAT STARTING POINT FOR A THRIVING PRAYER LIFE.

Let's wrap this week's devotion up by going back to the Scripture. Reread Philippians 1:1-11.

+ Is there anything we didn't cover that's striking your heart? Are there any verses that hit differently after reading this chapter?

I don't want to get too sappy here, but I have to admit . . . I'm praying for you! As your big sister in the faith, I'm so excited to see what God has in store for you through His Word!

As I read these first eleven verses of Philippians, I'm thanking God for you, the Delight girl who picked up this study, ready to grow in her faith. I pray with joy for you, my partner in the gospel and my teammate in God's mission for the world. I feel so confident that God who began a good work in you—the beautiful process of forming you into His image—will carry it on!

And, here's my final prayer as you embark on this journey God has in store for us through our study of Philippians. Why don't you join me in praying these words over the next season?

I pray that your love may abound more and more in knowledge and depth of insight, so that you may be able to discern what is best. May you be pure and blameless for the day of Christ, filled with the fruit of righteousness that comes through Christ Jesus, to the glory and praise of God.

Let's become wise old grandmas together!

PRAYERS & PRAISES

CONVERSATION

1. We're so excited to dive into our study of the book of Philippians! Consider . . . What are you hoping to learn from this study or this book of the Bible?

2. We are called to grow in love for our Creator and for the people around us. Which of these do you feel like you need the most help with these days? Why?

3. What's your prayer life like in this season of life? How would you like it to grow and mature by the end of this study?

4. Let's get super real . . . This study is about spiritual growth. If you're honest, do you really want to grow in your faith? What's been holding you back from growing?

02

WHAT'S MY PURPOSE?

What's My Purpose?

PHILIPPIANS 1:12-26

Have you heard the Billie Eilish smash hit "What Was I Made For?" I'm guessing we all played it really loudly in the car after the *Barbie* movie came out and cried semi-dramatically, staring out the window like we were in a music video. (Or was that just me?)

There's a reason that song won Song of the Year at the Grammy's, with lyrics surrounding the question of the meaning of life, a lack of purpose, a desire to matter . . . we all can relate. Honestly, it seems like the hot topic these days (outside of Christian circles as well as within them) is that search for purpose.

What's my calling? What's my purpose in life? What was I made for?

It's a question that blends well with our hopes for this study of Philippians. That search for direction is an obvious stop on the journey to faith development and spiritual growth. We're on the way to becoming all in for Jesus, so it makes sense that we'd desire clarity on what "all in" should look like for us as we're uniquely wired and created.

But, as we continue on in our reading of Paul's letter to the Philippians, I think we're going to find that the search for purpose is a little bit simpler and more straightforward than Billie Eilish makes it seem.

STOP & PRAY

LORD, I WANT TO SEEK YOU WITH ALL MY HEART. PLEASE SHOW ME YOUR PLAN FOR MY PURPOSE AND MY CALLING. OPEN MY EYES AND MY HEART AS I ENCOUNTER YOU THROUGH YOUR WORD.

01 YOUR PURPOSE IS CHRIST EXALTED

If anyone had a reason to doubt their God-given calling and that they were on track with God's plans for their life, it was Paul as he was writing this letter to the Philippians. If you remember from Chapter 1 we read Paul's opening prayer over his Philippian readers. He, very sweetly, asked God for their continued growth in their faith and love by God's power. Now, in verse 12, Paul switches gears and addresses the elephant in the room: the fact that he's writing to them from prison.

Go ahead and read Philippians 1:12-26.

+ Try to summarize what you just read in your own words in the space below.

NOTES:

We actually have a really cool window into what Paul's motivations might have been for addressing the imprisonment problem in his correspondence with the church in Philippi. In Acts 16:16-40, we read about the story of Paul and Silas in prison because of their defense of the gospel (the early Jesus followers often ruffled the feathers of the rulers of the day). In this epic moment, God miraculously freed them from their chains. Go ahead and flip there in your Bible if you're curious about the details!

But, guess where they were when this prison break happened . . .

+ FILL IN THE BLANK FROM ACTS 16:12.

"From there we traveled to ______________, a Roman colony and the leading city of that district of Macedonia. And we stayed there several days."

So the last time Paul was in Philippi, he was fantastically and miraculously rescued from certain death in a Roman jail cell. It was probably a much-repeated, highly revered story for the Philippian believers! And as you can imagine, it may have been confusing for them to hear that Paul was writing to them from another imprisonment, one God had not freed him from.

It begs the question: Why hadn't God rescued him from this prison as He had from the last one? One might assume that Paul was somehow outside of God's favor; clearly if he was operating in God's will, he wouldn't be locked up, right?

But it seems like Paul had a different perspective.

> *"Now I want you to know, brothers and sisters, that what has happened to me has actually served to advance the gospel. As a result, it has become clear throughout the whole palace guard and to everyone else that I am in chains for Christ. And because of my chains, most of the brothers and sisters have become confident in the Lord and dare all the more to proclaim the gospel without fear."*
> *Philippians 1:12–14 (emphasis added)*

You see, Paul's life purpose wasn't success or freedom or comfort. To Paul, every part of his life was a means to an end: glorification and exaltation of the God he was in love with and the Savior he believed in. The fact that he was in jail couldn't possibly hold him back from that purpose! In fact, it helped it and spurred it on, just as he details in verses 12-14 as he describes the new faith of the palace guards and the strengthening of his fellow believers in the Lord.

+ FILL IN THE BLANKS FROM PHILIPPIANS 1:20.

"I eagerly expect and hope that I will in no way be ashamed, but will have sufficient courage so that now as always ________ ________ ________ ________ in my body, whether by life or by death."

I think our purpose in life is the same as Paul's: We are here on earth to see Christ exalted. Our true and highest purpose is to allow as much praise, honor, worship, and fame for Jesus to bubble up through our earthly lives as we can. And, if you think about it, that purpose is a lot simpler than a lifelong journey of trying to discern the "path" God has for us. If our purpose is Christ exalted, we can fulfill that anywhere and anyhow.

If your purpose is Christ exalted, you can be fulfilled and full at your dream school or at the community college down the road.

If your purpose is Christ exalted, you can be on mission whether you're in love with your major or you aren't.

If your purpose is Christ exalted, then suddenly there's no longer such a thing as a "roadblock" to your true calling. *Here and now is the best place to see Jesus praised!*

+ Let's make sure we're all on the same page here . . . What's your purpose in life?

OK, OK . . . I know what you might be thinking right now. *I get that my purpose is to exalt Christ, but what does that have to do with how I live my day to day life? What does it mean for me tangibly as I'm trying to discern God's path for my life? How do I know if I'm on the right track with where He wants to lead me and what He wants me to do?*

Trust me girl, I've been in your shoes! For most of my life, I was 100 percent certain my calling and my purpose was to be a worship leader at a church. And, after pursuing a worship leadership major at my Nashville dream school 700 miles away from home, I really thought I'd "made it." I was living the dream, both my dream for myself and what I thought was God's dream for me.

Then, when I got hit with a mysterious chronic illness that nobody could figure out, when my parents called me two weeks before my freshman fall semester ended to tell me they weren't comfortable with me being so sick and so far away, when I had to transfer to the local community college for a semester, and when I landed at a random university 30 minutes from home in Texas for my sophomore year of college with a biology major (because, why not?), I was *crushed.*

You see, I was absolutely sure my purpose was in Nashville at that school with that specific major. I thought that this illness, my parents' decision, and my new "direction" represented a complete derailment of all the plans God had for me. I was convinced that this was a disobedient pit stop, and that God's dreams for me were on hold until I could get my act together and get with the program.

But here's the thing: *I was wrong!*

02 THERE'S STILL PURPOSE IN THE FIRE

Reread Philippians 1:15-20.

Remember, Paul's *in jail* writing this! That's the definition of derailed plans! God had called him to preach the Good News of the gospel to the Gentiles. If you and I were in his shoes, we'd be chomping at the bit to get out of prison, shut down those competitive other pastors, and get going on our real purpose. But somehow Paul seems just as fired up with the ministry that's happening—the exalting of Jesus—while he's seemingly "off track" as he would be if he were free and back in Philippi with his friends.

> *"But what does it matter? The important thing is that in every way, whether from false motives or true, Christ is preached. And because of this I rejoice."*
> *Philippians 1:18*

This whole idea of the wrong place being the right place in God's eyes reminds me of another Bible story, one you may or may not be familiar with. Flip backwards in your Bible to Daniel 3 and read the story of Shadrach, Meshach, and Abednego.

Stories like this really put things into perspective, don't they? I thought my life was over because I had to go to school in Texas instead of Tennessee and I threw a fit that lasted at least a year. These guys were thrown into a *literal blazing furnace* for living out their purpose of loving God with all they've got, and somehow they were still on mission—even in the face of death.

+ FILL IN THE BLANKS BELOW FROM DANIEL 3:16-18.

"Shadrach, Meshach and Abednego replied to him, 'King Nebuchadnezzar, we do not need to defend ourselves before you in this matter. If we are thrown into the blazing furnace, the God we serve is able to deliver us from it, and he will deliver us from Your Majesty's hand. ________ ________

________ ________ ________ ________,

we want you to know, Your Majesty, that we will not serve your gods or worship the image of gold you have set up.'"

But even if He does not . . . This is so convicting! Are you so sure of your own perspective of where you should be and where God has you that your eyes are closed to how He might want to move in the here and now? Are you sulking in a "derailed" season that God might actually have purpose for you in? Are you so convinced that God's going to work one way that you're blind to the alternative route He may be guiding you along?

Maybe we should be a little bit more like Paul and a little bit more like those men in the furnace–trusting that God's good plans can't be stopped by a little bit of jailtime, a blazing inferno, or even a university transfer.

That's what I learned in my furnace season. Even though He did not bring me back to that school in Nashville, and even though He did not restore me to that worship leadership major, and even though He did not move in the way I expected . . . *there was still purpose in the fire!*

It was there in that 30-minutes-from-home college apartment where God miraculously healed me from my years-long sickness. It was there where he led me to start a Delight chapter with some friendly strangers that led to many women giving their lives to Jesus for the first time. It was there that He set me on a path that would eventually lead me back to Nashville doing a job that was over and above anything I could have dreamed up for myself.

What if where you are right now is where God intended you to be?

Think It Through

+ **Can you think of a time where you felt "derailed" in your purpose? What was it like?**

+ **Can you pinpoint any unexpected ways God moved or was exalted in that season?**

Alrighty, let's land this plane ladies! So we know our purpose in life is to exalt Christ (Are you sick of me repeating that yet? No? Great!) and we know that nothing can get in the way of that, not even a fiery furnace or a Roman jail. But what about our *calling?* What about the dreams God has for us, the avenue through which He has planned for us to achieve our purpose?

To find out what our calling is, we'll need to jump back to this week's Scripture one last time.

Reread Philippians 1:21-26.

+ **Which verse stands out to you the most from this section?**

This is some of the most striking discourse in the entire New Testament. Paul's thought process here is *incredible.* Certainly none of us have reached the level of spiritual maturity and wisdom to be able to say the kinds of things he writes here!

"For to me, to live is Christ and to die is gain."
Philippians 1:21

Paul writes with passion about his hope to be with Jesus and his eager expectation of the unity with Christ he'll find in Heaven. For Paul, that's the prize. In fact, he *wants* to die so he can go be with Jesus. The Greek word he uses in verse 23 to describe his desire is one of passionate longing, a desperate thirst. But somehow he concludes that, though being with Jesus would be better, serving the church in pursuit of the gospel and the glorification of Christ on Earth is "necessary." So he's convinced his time for Heaven hasn't quite come yet.

Can you see where we're going with this? Yes, Paul's passion and purpose was Jesus, Jesus, and Jesus. But his calling—his day to day mission while on Earth—was one of *obedience.*

03 Your Calling Is Daily Obedience

+ Look back at Philippians 1:25 in your Bible and underline "for your progress and joy in the faith."

Here's a reminder we all need: Jesus is coming back soon. He's going to make all things new, uniting Heaven and Earth and bringing His beloved children back to perfect unity with Him. But, until then, *we've got work to do!*

Do you have a girl on your dorm floor who doesn't know about Jesus? Then you've got work to do!

Do you have Christian community in need of support, prayer, and encouragement in their faith? Then you've got work to do!

NOTES:

Do you have further to go in your search for God, in your desire to know and love Him more fully? Then you've got work to do!

It's as simple and tangible as it can possibly get. If you're still here on Earth and if Jesus hasn't returned by the time you're reading this chapter, then your calling is to take the next right step of obedience wherever God is leading you. Your calling is to do what God asks you to do, when He asks you to do it.

That obedience may bring you to a certain major, into a certain conversation, or through a certain trial. It may cause you some discomfort, it may stretch you, and it might even grow you. This obedience—always stemming from the true and perfect Word of God and from the whispers of the Holy Spirit—will call you deeper into your faith journey, baby step by baby step.

+ What's one simple step of obedience to God you could take today? (Ex: reading your Bible, praying over a friend, inviting a coworker to church, confessing a sin . . . etc)

KEEP GROWING

IT CAN BE HARD TO STAY ON TRACK WITH DAILY OBEDIENCE WHEN WE GET CAUGHT UP IN THE FAST-PACED WHIRLWIND OF LIFE. ONE OF OUR FAVORITE WAYS TO STAY ON MISSION IS THROUGH ACCOUNTABILITY. ARE YOU FEELING CALLED TO DAILY OBEDIENCE? FIND A GOD-FEARING FRIEND WHO CAN CHECK IN ON YOUR PROGRESS AND HELP HOLD YOU ACCOUNTABLE IN YOUR PURPOSE OF EXALTING GOD IN EVERYTHING YOU DO.

My husband says it like this: *My business is to live as long as I can, as well as I can, to serve my master as faithfully as I can, until He sees fit to call me home.*

King David said it like this:

> *"Hope in the Lord and keep his way. He will exalt you to inherit the land . . . "*
> *Psalm 37:34*

As children of God, we know what we're made for. We're made to love and honor God in every circumstance. We were made to serve His Kingdom and His mission with all we've got. And we get to do all of this with an eternal perspective: that one day we get to be with Him face to face.

PRAYERS & PRAISES

CONVERSATION

1. College is the time where we're encouraged—or even pressured—to discover our purpose in life. How have you experienced this in your time in college?

2. Can you think of a time where Christ was exalted through your life or through the life of someone you know? What was it like?

3. Are you in a fire right now? How might the story of Shadrach, Meshach, and Abednego change the way you view it or respond to it?

4. Our calling in life is to daily obedience. Flip back to page 47 and find the simple step of obedience you want to take. What's your plan for making it happen? Why did you choose that one in particular?

03

WHAT IF I'M NOT HUMBLE?

What If I'm Not Humble?

PHILIPPIANS 1:27 - 2:4

My deepest sin struggles are selfishness and pride.

Genuinely, I think I'm the most selfish person I know. I've been a little bit too "main character energy" since I was little, always thinking of my own wants first and allowing the wants and needs of others to get pushed to an afterthought. It's a habit I've tried to break for many years in my adult life, but even now it creeps up in my day-to-day, as much as I'd like to say I've overcome it.

And don't even get me started on pride . . . It's yucky and icky and nasty and it has deep, deep roots in my heart. Though God constantly puts me in situations that humble me and remind me of my faults and my need for Him, my first instinct is still to assume I'm better than the gal next to me; that I'm smarter, that I could do what she does more efficiently, or even that I'm "further along" in my faith than her.

Is it OK that I'm being real with you right now? I bet there are some of you reading this who can't relate. Your poison comes in different forms; pride or selfishness don't often trip you up. *But I also think these are the sneaky sins,* the ones we don't love to admit at Bible study and the ones we're nervous to even write down in our prayer journals for fear of discovery. There may be some of you reading this who know just what I mean when I say I'm prideful and selfish. You, too, listen to a sermon and consider how you would have preached it better. You, too, secretly love when you finish a test first or when you're the friend group's go-to for life advice.

This is an uncomfortable conversation, I know! And I think Paul knew that, too, when he brought it up in this next portion of Philippians. But we'll see as we read that it's also a *necessary* conversation, especially if we want to grow as children of God–especially if we crave the holy unity Paul describes all throughout the book.

So I'm committing to vulnerability this week and I think you should join me. Let's allow our walls to come down and give the Holy Spirit permission to work on even the messiest parts of our inner lives. I truly believe God has something powerful for us on the other side of this!

STOP & PRAY

LORD, YOU HAVE FULL PERMISSION TO ADDRESS ANY SELFISHNESS OR PRIDE THAT I HAVE ALLOWED TO TAKE ROOT IN MY HEART. I WANT TO PURSUE YOU IN PURITY AND UNITY WITH THE COMMUNITY YOU HAVE PLACED IN MY LIFE. SHOW ME HOW TO SURRENDER WHAT I HOLD TOO TIGHTLY ONTO AND HOW TO EMBRACE YOUR HUMBLE AND SACRIFICIAL WAY OF LIVING.

To start this off, let's go ahead and finish out the last bit of chapter 1 left over from last week. Stop and read Philippians 1:27-30.

+ FILL IN THE BLANK FROM PHILIPPIANS 1:27.

"Whatever happens, conduct yourselves in a manner worthy of the gospel of Christ. Then, whether I come and see you or only hear about you in my absence, I will know that you __________ __________ in the __________ Spirit, striving __________ as __________ for the faith of the gospel…"

NOTES:

Paul's goal for us as we grow in our faith, a goal we'll see repeated all throughout Philippians, is that we would *stand firm in unity under the gospel of Jesus Christ.* That's the "life worthy of the gospel" he's calling us to.

+ Now, find Philippians 2:1 in your Bible and circle the first word.

I've been taught that every time you see a "therefore" in the Bible, it should prompt you to consider what it's "there for." In this instance, it's pretty clear: Paul's calling us to unity. *Therefore* we need to follow Jesus's example of humility. Gospel unity is a byproduct of godly humility.

Here's the ugly truth: There's no greater roadblock to the ideal Christian unity God has for us than our own self-centeredness. Oof. Convicting? Definitely!

+ Before we get further along in this conversation, stop and evaluate your heart . . . How do you feel about the whole "humility" conversation? Do you struggle with pride or selfishness?

Alright, now let's get cracking on the first few verses of chapter 2, our main focus for this week.

Go ahead and read Philippians 2:1-2.

In my research over this portion of Scripture, I read a commentary from a theologian who described Paul's intro here as "obvious" points, a rhetorical device to hook his readers into the heart behind what he was saying. "He could have just as easily said, 'If water is wet, if fire is hot, if rocks are hard,' and so forth,"[1] the theologian says. Paul is reminding the Philippians (and us, too!) of the many "benefits" we've received as children of God, adopted into the family of Christ.

+ What are the "benefits" of life with Christ Paul lists in Philippians 2:1?

But what do these "benefits" of Christ's encouragement, comfort, love, His Spirit, tenderness, and compassion have to do with humility? It's that *we don't deserve them!* Sister, the way Jesus loves you should humble you daily.

01 HUMILITY STARTS AT THE FEET OF JESUS

There's a beautiful story repeated a few different times in the Gospels that illustrates this point (that a humble heart stems from acknowledgement of what Jesus has done for us). Flip to Luke 7:36-50 in your Bible and read through it.

Essentially, this woman—widely regarded as a "sinner"—crashed a dinner party Jesus was at and washed His feet with her hair and her tears, dumping perfume all over Him. It was an extravagant and frankly *embarrassing* expression of her passionate love and gratitude for Jesus, a move that made all the other people in the room pretty uncomfortable.

Jesus, however, saw her sacrifice for what it was: humble worship.

"Then he turned toward the woman and said to Simon, 'Do you see this woman? I came into your house. You did not give me any water for my feet, but she wet my feet with her tears and wiped them with her hair. You did not give me a kiss, but this woman, from the time I entered, has not stopped kissing my feet. You did not put oil on my head, but she has poured perfume on my feet. Therefore, I tell you, her many sins have been forgiven—as her great love has shown. But whoever has been forgiven little loves little.'"

Luke 7:44–47 (emphasis added)

It's a stark comparison. The woman who is so clearly and intimately aware of the grace Jesus has lavished on her is moved to acts of worship that make her look like a fool to any outside observer. But, the Pharisees and others watching who had perhaps forgotten of the "benefits" of life with Jesus were moved to judge her. They, in their pride, saw themselves as above this sinful woman, therefore missing out on a holy encounter with Jesus.

NOTES:

This is the danger! If we're not careful to constantly bring ourselves back to the feet of Jesus and to consistently meditate on the undeserved grace and forgiveness He's freely given us, we are going to end up like those Pharisees time and time again.

When we forget the way God had to swoop in and rescue us from that porn addiction, we're more prone to judge the girl in our small group who's sleeping with her boyfriend.

When we forget the forgiveness God gave us a year ago when we didn't deserve it, we are more prone to withhold forgiveness from that family member who hurt us.

When we forget just how far Jesus has taken us on our journey of faith, we are more prone to put ourselves "above" a fellow believer who hasn't accomplished as much.

If you find yourself struggling with pride in this season, perhaps it's because you forgot just how little you deserve *anything* that God has given you. Maybe you've forgotten just how good God really is. Let this be an invitation . . . All it takes is a moment at His feet (maybe with some tears and some perfume) to receive a fresh perspective, one that's a little more humble.

THINK IT THROUGH

+ Be honest . . . Can you think of a time where you were like the Pharisees from the story in Luke 7? Describe it below.

+ Has there ever been a time where you were humbled at the feet of Jesus like the sinful woman? What was that like?

Now, the next two verses of Philippians 2 are even more culture-breaking and subversive than what came before. Check it out!

> *"Do nothing out of selfish ambition or vain conceit. Rather, in humility value others above yourselves, not looking to your own interests but each of you to the interests of the others."*
> *Philippians 2:3–4*

If you were to drop these verses casually in a 21st century conversation, you'd probably get some wild looks. Today's culture is all about self love, self care, self esteem, "girl bossing" your way to the top, doing what's best for you . . . The truth of the matter is that it's not popular to "value others above yourselves." In fact, we're told it's actually *toxic* to do that, that preserving our self image is high-priority.

So if what Paul's saying here is true, that God's design is for all of us to view others as more important than ourselves, then we're in for a little bit of culture shock.

02 SHE'S MORE IMPORTANT THAN ME

This kind of selflessness Paul describes doesn't come naturally to me. It's a lesson I've had to relearn over and over. One moment that stands out in my mind actually has to do with these Delight books. A few years ago, my friend was working on a cover design for one of our studies. She happens to be one of my favorite people on the planet but, remember, I also happen to be incredibly selfish and particular. So, when she sent me a cover design that didn't match what I'd made up in my head, I threw a fit.

I remember calling my boss to complain that I didn't like it, genuinely thinking she'd take my side. But her response shook me to my core and, honestly, helped form me into the person I am today.

What's more important to you? That you like the cover, or that she feels honored in her design skills?

Gut. Punch.

The wise advice hit me like a ton of bricks because I'd gotten so caught up in myself—in my preferences, my likes, my thoughts, my opinions—that I'd decided what *I* wanted was more important than this person who I loved so much and who God loved even more than I did. In my own "selfish ambition" and "vain conceit" I looked to my own interests, not the interests of others, which is exactly what Philippians 2 warns us against.

And, this message of selflessness isn't just contained to the book of Philippians. It's repeated and emphasized all across the Bible!

+ FILL IN THE BLANKS BELOW FROM ROMANS 12:10.

"Be devoted to one another in love. __________ one another __________ yourselves."

+ FILL IN THE BLANKS BELOW FROM LUKE 9:23.

"Then he said to them all: 'Whoever wants to be my disciple must ______________ ______________ and take up their cross daily and follow me.'"

+ FILL IN THE BLANKS BELOW FROM LUKE 9:23.

"No one should seek their ______________ good, but the good of ______________."

+ Can you find any other Bible verses teaching about selflessness? (It's OK if you need to use Google. We won't judge!)

You might not be put into the situation of deciding between your own preference and a coworker's preference when designing a Bible study, but I can guarantee opportunities to honor someone above yourself will come up in your life. What about when you get in an argument with a friend and you have to be the one who apologizes first, even when it really was her fault? What about when you get asked to serve an extra service in the kid's ministry at your church even when it infringes on your brunch plans? What about . . . Well, you get it! Fill in the blanks!

KEEP GROWING

Check out this quote from the "Enduring Word" Bible commentary and consider... How might my little acts of selflessness actually have a huge impact on the unity of my community?

"THIS REBUKES MUCH OF THE CULTURE'S CONCEPT OF SELF-ESTEEM . . . AS WE ESTEEM OTHERS BETTER, WE WILL NATURALLY HAVE A CONCERN FOR THEIR NEEDS AND CONCERNS. THIS SORT OF OUTWARD LOOKING MENTALITY NATURALLY LEADS TO A UNITY AMONG THE PEOPLE OF GOD. IF I CONSIDER YOU ABOVE ME AND YOU CONSIDER ME ABOVE YOU, THEN A MARVELOUS THING HAPPENS: WE HAVE A COMMUNITY WHERE EVERYONE IS LOOKED UP TO, AND NO ONE IS LOOKED DOWN ON."[2]

Yes, humbling yourself by elevating the people around you is culturally subversive, but it's also one of the simplest ways to imitate Christ! How beautiful would it be if all of us committed to finding opportunities in our day to take the low place and put someone else first?! I think it would feel refreshing, unifying, and *holy*.

+ Brainstorm! What's one way you can honor someone above yourself this week?

Alrighty! Let's look at this whole chunk of the Bible holistically as we wrap things up for this week. Reread Philippians 1:27 – 2:4.

We've gotta keep Paul's greater message in mind. We're not just learning humility and selflessness so we can become "better Christians." These spiritual practices have a greater purpose, one of unity *within* the body of Christ and impact *through* the body of Christ.

03 Our Unity, Humility, & Selflessness Spurs on the Gospel of Jesus

I read a quote about this that made me want to reevaluate my whole life . . . Let's see if you feel the same way when you read it!

"In all ages—and not least today—the greatest hindrance to the advance of the gospel has been the inconsistency of Christians." [3]

Gosh, if you think about it, this couldn't be more true! The people I know who are skeptical of the whole "Jesus" thing feel that way for good reason. They see people professing passionate love for Christ in their Instagram bio's, then bashing a certain political party on their stories. They hear Christians declare that "God is love" then watch as we fail to love even other Christians like God would. They hear enough of the Bible to know Christians are supposed to be different, then we act just like the rest of the world.

It's a sobering thought . . . But, it's also an incredible opportunity!

What if we actually took Paul's words to heart? What if we actually did "conduct [ourselves] in a manner worthy of the gospel of Christ" (Philippians 1:27)? What if we truly were "like-minded, having the same love, being one in spirit and of one mind" (Philippians 2:2)? What if we really could "do nothing out of selfish ambition or vain conceit" (Philippians 2:3)?

I don't think it's wild to say that children of God actually living out God's design of humble worship, radical selflessness, and holy unity would start a revolution of faith that could stir up revival in every corner of the world, beginning right where you are: on your campus, in your classes, and in your dorm room.

And do you wanna know the best part? *We don't have to do it alone!*

+ Look back at Philippians 1:27 – 2:4 in your Bible and underline every time God's "Spirit" is mentioned.

God knows we're selfish. God knows we're prideful. God knows our sinful patterns lead us more toward disunity than unity. So He sent us Himself: a helper, comforter, and encourager who chooses to dwell inside of us when we give our lives to Jesus. The Holy Spirit of God can and *will* empower you every day in your journey toward living a life worthy of the gospel of Christ. You have a companion every step of the way, nudging you in the right direction, pointing you to Scripture, and strengthening you in your weakest moments!

What a gift!

So this week, as you practice God's design for humility, invite the Holy Spirit into it. He can turn an unnatural spiritual discipline into a joy, something as easy as breathing.

And trust me, I'm preaching to myself here! Maybe I'm not the most selfish person I know (and perhaps I should stop saying that about myself). Maybe I'm just a sinful girl who has been given a radical gift of grace. God's still working on me bit by bit. I think He's happy to do the same for you!

Let's take the next step in this journey of faith together.

PRAYERS & PRAISES

CONVERSATION

1. Alright, let's get real. Do you ever struggle with pride or selfishness? How does it show up in your life?

2. Consider the story from Luke 7 about the woman who poured perfume on Jesus's feet. What stands out to you most from that Scripture? What does it teach you about Jesus's character?

3. Can you think of a time when someone honored you above themselves? What was it like? How did it make you feel?

4. The Holy Spirit helps us in our journey toward godly humility. What step do you feel called to take in your own humility journey after reading this chapter?

04

WHY JESUS?

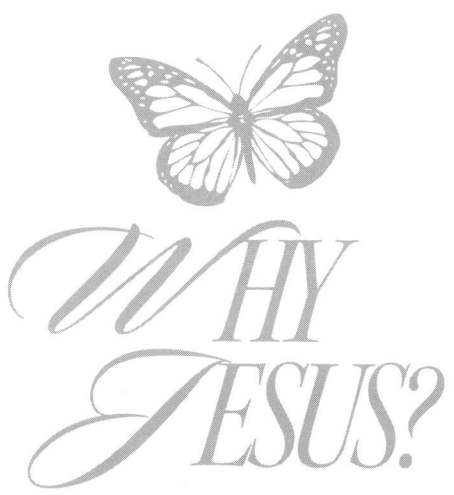

WHY JESUS?

PHILIPPIANS 2:5-11

Imagine the book of Philippians as an atom. So far we've been hanging out in the electron cloud, exploring ideas that are in Paul's orbit. We've studied spiritual growth, purpose, and humility–important parts of the Christian walk for those of us who want to go deeper, though not necessarily central or crucial for the lifeblood of what God's heart is for us. But this week we get to the nucleus of his message, the core of the book that every other portion revolves around. If you removed this part, everything else would fall out of alignment.

For Paul, everything is centered on the gospel of Jesus.

Read Philippians 2:5-11.

This portion of Scripture, known as "The Messiah Poem," is the core of Paul's arguments and message for the Philippian church. It's the heart and gospel and mission of Jesus wrapped up in a beautiful bow. This week, we're going to meditate on these words and explore what they mean for us.

+ Take some time to meditate on Philippians 2:5-11 on your own. Take notes on what stands out to you, try praying it out loud, and draw your own conclusions about what God might be saying to us through this Scripture.

In each chapter of our study up to this point, we've attempted to answer important questions we face in our lives and faith journeys. So far we've hit: "How do I grow?", "What's my purpose?", and "What if I'm not humble?" But as hard-hitting as those conversations were, I think this one is the most important. It's the question every single one of us faces when deciding whether or not to give Jesus our everything, when determining what route our lives will take, or discerning what to believe or not believe.

Why Jesus?

For the girl who grew up in a Christian home, this is the thought that pops up when you start to question your parents' religion for the first time. Whether it's doubt or deconstruction, we've all thought it at one time or another . . . *Why Jesus?*

For the girl who encountered Christianity later in life and is just starting to get to know what this faith thing is all about in college, it's the question on the forefront of your mind as you consider whether you're in or out . . . *Why Jesus?*

Even for the girl who's sure of her eternity in Heaven, this question rears its head when trial or tragedy strikes; when you pray hard but that family member still dies, when following God leads you down the path less traveled toward persecution or pain . . . *Why Jesus?*

Here's the goal: no matter where you're starting from, by the end of this chapter you'll be just as certain as Paul is about who Jesus is and why He's worthy of your everything.

STOP & PRAY

LORD, REVEAL THE POWER OF YOUR GOSPEL TO ME IN A FRESH WAY AS I READ YOUR WORD.

OK, let's take this chunk of Scripture bit by bit. If you remember from last week, Paul was teaching the Philippian church that humility is the key to unity. We're picking up at what one might assume is the end of that thought, but it's actually a clever buildup to the main event of the whole book.

+ FILL IN THE BLANKS BELOW FROM PHILIPPIANS 2:5.

"In your relationships with one another, have the ____________ ____________ as ____________ ____________ . . ."

Think of this line as the short flash of lightning right before the biggest thunderclap you've ever heard in your life. Paul, commenting on his call to humility, narrows in on the key.

It's simple. *Have the same mindset as Jesus.* It's a call all throughout the Bible that asks us to look more like Christ every day and grow in holiness—the whole purpose of this study!

But, in reality it's not simple at all. You see, I'm 20+ years into my walk with the Lord and most parts of me still don't look much like Him at all. Which brings us to our first point:

01 YOU NEED JESUS

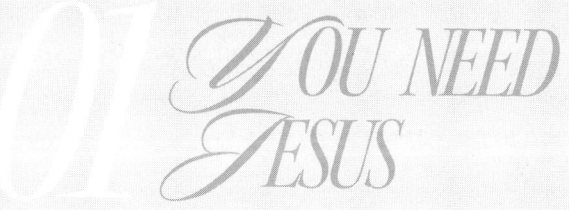

Have you ever tried your best at something (like, really gave it your all) only to still fail at the end? Maybe you studied the hardest you'd ever studied before for that big test but still found yourself with the lowest grade in the class. Maybe you put your whole heart into saving that relationship only to get hit with an out of nowhere breakup the week before Christmas.

That's what we're like when we try to "have the same mindset as Christ." As hard as we try, as much effort as we put in, as good as our intentions are, we still find ourselves missing the mark again and again. That's why Paul's call to a heavenly state of mind isn't as simple as it seems. For those of us who've lived life in the real world, we know just how impossible it is.

Paul explains it this way in his letter to the Romans.

"...for all have sinned and fall short of the glory of God..."
Romans 3:23

It's a losing battle no matter how you slice it. Without the power of Jesus, we cannot ever hope to be *like* Jesus. And that's the hangup! Because only someone as perfect as Jesus could earn their way into Heaven.

Think of the very best person you know. They've loved the Lord for years, they have the whole Bible memorized, they're humble, wise, and pure. That person, as good as they seem by our standards, is still miles and miles away from God's perfection. They're still so stained by sin they could never hope to stand in the presence of a holy God. Eternal separation from God is still their only option.

Even the best person you know could never save themselves. *The only One who could save us is Jesus.*

Check out the very next verse from Romans 2!

"... and all are justified freely by his grace through the redemption that came by Christ Jesus."
Romans 3:24

Jesus came to redeem broken people who could never live up to the Heavenly standard. Through His grace, and only through His grace, can we stand face to face with God Almighty and have a home in Heaven when we die.

So, *why Jesus?* Because we need Him! No one else can save you but Jesus.

THINK IT THROUGH

+ **Be honest . . . On a scale of 1-10, how confident are you that you're going to Heaven when you die?**

1 |—|—|—|—|—|—|—|—|—| 10

+ **Why did you answer that way?**

If you answered anything less than a 10 to the question above, I have great news for you. You can be 100 percent sure *today*. Let's keep reading in Philippians to find out how.

Read Philippians 2:6-8.

The simple gospel of Jesus Christ is this: that God chose to send His only Son to live a perfect yet painful life on Earth. That Son, Jesus, would go on to die a horrific death on a cross as the sacrifice for our sin and brokenness. And through that sacrifice, He defeated death and the devil and was raised again, offering all who would call on His name an avenue for redemption and reunion with God and a room in Heaven when we die. Where there was no way, there is one now, thanks to Jesus and His great love for us.

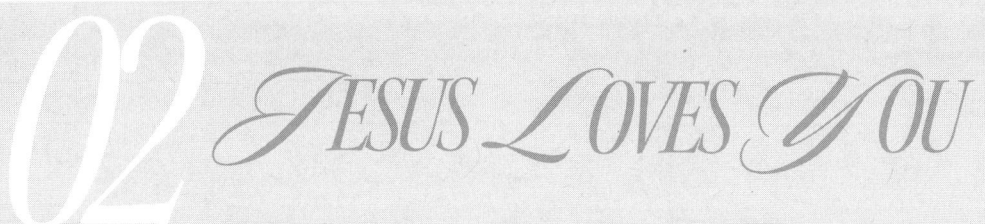

02 Jesus Loves You

Somehow, though, we've managed to sugarcoat that gospel story. We've accidentally watered it down, making it feel normal and palatable. But, when we read verses like Paul's poem in Philippians 2, that "normalness" should be thrown out the window.

> *"... rather, [Jesus] made himself nothing..."*
> *Philippians 2:7a*

"... he humbled himself by becoming obedient to death—even death on a cross!"
Philippians 2:8b

Jesus is *God*! He's always existed, in perfection and glory, from the very beginning. But for some wild reason, He *chose* to be born into a broken world as a baby, the picture of helplessness. He *chose* to live and grow in a world filled with grief and tragedy. He *chose* to die, brutally and terribly. And somehow, the motivation for that decision was you and me.

Last week we learned that the way Jesus loves us should humble us. And here again, that love needs to be our starting point. It's so backwards and upside down that a holy God would empty Himself for broken people. The only reason He would is the greatest reason of all: because He purely, tenderly, and passionately loves us, even at our very worst.

+ FILL IN THE BLANK FROM 1 JOHN 4:9-10.

"This is how God showed his ___________ among us: He sent his one and only Son into the world that we might live through him. This is __________ : not that we loved God, but that __________ ___________ __________ and sent his Son as an atoning sacrifice for our sins."

In His love, you became worth dying for. In His love, you became worth any sacrifice. The question stirring in our hearts begins to morph from *Why Jesus?* to *Why me?*

+ Flip through your Bible or use Google to find other verses referencing God's love for us. (John 3:16 and Romans 5:8 are great starting points!)

Meditating on the great love Jesus has for you, on the ultimate sacrifice He thought you were worth, brings you closer and closer, bit by bit, to a true understanding of the gospel. As we meditate on Jesus's love expressed through the gospel story, the less likely we become to water it down or forget the real impact. I believe the more we reflect on the humble and mighty love of Jesus, the more natural it will feel to fall into His arms, whether for the very first time or in a fresh wave of surrender.

You see, no one could love you like Jesus. When we know that really and truly, there's no other option that makes sense other than giving your whole heart to Him.

+ Take a moment to meditate on Jesus's love for you, using this week's Scripture as a starting point. Write down your prayers, thoughts, or reflections below!

The coolest part of Paul's poem is next. Let's read it together.

> *"Therefore God exalted him to the highest place*
> *and gave him the name that is above every name,*
> *that at the name of Jesus every knee should bow,*
> *in heaven and on earth and under the earth,*
> *and every tongue acknowledge that Jesus Christ is*
> *Lord, to the glory of God the Father."*
> *Philippians 2:9-11*

Why *Jesus?* Because one day, every knee will bow.

03 JESUS IS LORD

After describing Jesus's humble sacrifice and His willing death for our redemption, Paul uses the second half of his Savior hymn to describe Jesus's eternal victory.

KEEP GROWING

DID YOU KNOW THAT BIBLICAL AUTHORS OFTEN REFERENCE OTHER PARTS OF THE BIBLE IN THEIR WRITINGS? PAUL'S DOING THAT HERE BY QUOTING ISAIAH 45 TO DESCRIBE WHAT IT WILL LOOK LIKE WHEN WE'RE FACE TO FACE WITH JESUS.

LOOK UP ISAIAH 45:22-23 TO CHECK IT OUT FOR YOURSELF!

These verses beautifully illustrate the "upside down-ness" of the gospel of Jesus. Somehow, in humbling Himself and choosing the low path (v 6-8), God exalted Jesus and gave Him the highest honor (v 9-11). It's the same way for us when we give our lives to Him! We go low: confessing our sins, admitting our need for God's rescue, and calling out for His help. Then, God gives us the greatest gift: His mercy, forgiveness, and an eternal home in Heaven.

So here's the thing: God is God and Jesus is Lord whether we acknowledge it or not.

Jesus is Lord even if you spend your whole life denying it or ignoring it or searching for proof.

Christ is king whether you acknowledge His hand at work in your life or not.

God is God no matter who else or what else your heart decides to cling to.

> *"Salvation is found in no one else, for there is no other name under heaven given to mankind by which we must be saved."*
> *Acts 4:12*

Between writing this chapter and the one before it, I gave birth to my first baby, a perfect, wonderful little girl. Loving her and being her mom makes this whole gospel conversation seem even more vital than it ever has.

NOTES:

You see, she could go her whole life denying Jesus. She could hear about His sacrifice for her, learn about His love for her, and still decide she wants no part of it. She could reject His plans and His good gifts and His affection and live a life separate from Him.

Then, when she's 100 years old, it could click. She could finally decide to stop running and give her life to Jesus on her deathbed. In an instant, she would be forgiven and be welcomed into Heaven with open arms.

But, Heaven's pleasures set aside, what a sad thing it would be for her to live her whole earthly life without Jesus. She'd miss out on secret conversations with her maker in her college dorm room in the early hours of the morning.

She'd miss out on spiritual gifts He had planned for her and ways she could make a huge impact for His Kingdom. She'd miss out on godly community, the comfort of the Holy Spirit, and the endless wonders found in her Bible. She'd miss out on true joy, peace, and fulfillment.

That's what I want for my daughter! An earthly life spent hand in hand with Jesus and an eternal life by His side. And I believe it's God's heart for you, too.

If you've never given your life to Him, or if you can't or won't give a confident 10 to your eternal destination, God doesn't want you to waste another minute. He wants your messiest thoughts, your early mornings, and your whole heart. He wants to reveal His love to you. You could give Him your everything today.

Or if you've found yourself in the midst of tragedy and got out of step with the fire and passion for Christ you first had, His call to you is the same. He has more to show you, more love to lavish on you, and new paths to lead you on. You could give Him your everything today.

If you're lukewarm in your faith, angry at God, too busy, or feeling forgotten, you could give Him your everything today.

Why Jesus? Because you need Him, because He loves you, and because your forever could start right now.

Prayers & Praises

CONVERSATION

1. Are you 100 percent confident that you're going to Heaven when you die? Why or why not? If you aren't 100 percent confident right now, what do you think it would take to get you there?

2. When was the last time you were reminded of how much you need Jesus? Describe it below.

3. Re-read 1 John 4:9-10. What stands out to you from those verses? What do they teach you about Jesus, God, or the Holy Spirit? What do they reveal to you about the gospel?

4. Does Jesus have your everything? What area of your life do you feel called to allow Jesus to be Lord over in this season?

05

HOW CAN I LIVE SET APART

HOW CAN I LIVE SET APART

PHILIPPIANS 2:12-30

I don't know about you, but I have been *loving* our time spent together in the book of Philippians. It feels like we've just begun to scratch the surface of the hidden mysteries this letter from Paul holds. But somehow, we're already halfway through our study!

We're coming off a major high from last week; Philippians 2:6-11 is some of the most beautiful, poetic writing in the whole New Testament. The message it holds (the gospel!) is even more beautiful. In fact, I think we need to revisit Paul's "Messiah Poem" one more time.

+ Find Philippians 2:6-11 in your Bible and read it out loud.

KEEP GROWING

DID YOU KNOW YOU CAN PRAY SCRIPTURE? TRY READING BIBLE VERSES OUT LOUD AS IF YOU WERE PRAYING THEM (PSALMS ARE A GREAT PLACE TO START WITH THIS!). IT'S A GREAT TOOL TO GROW YOUR PRAYER LIFE OR TO HELP YOUR BIBLE READING TIME FEEL FRESH. WHAT BETTER WAY TO TALK TO GOD THAN BY SPEAKING HIS OWN WORDS BACK TO HIM?!

Verse 12 kicks things off for our study this week with a classic "therefore." Now, remember, whenever we see a "therefore," we need to stop and ask ourselves what it's there for. In this case, it's a connector. Paul's working to bring not only the Messiah Poem, but all of his arguments in chapter 2 together. First he highlighted Christ's humility (like we learned about in Chapter 3 of our study) and now he's going to land the plane by emphasizing Christ's *obedience.*

And, as we've come to expect from Paul, he's going to call his readers to emulate Jesus's example.

Go ahead and read Philippians 2:12-18.

STOP & PRAY

GOD, THANK YOU FOR YOUR WORD AND YOUR EXAMPLE IN CHRIST. SHOW US HOW TO BE MORE LIKE YOU AS WE SEEK YOUR HEART.

Christians have lots of cutesy little sayings; phrases affectionately dubbed "Christianese." They're helpful for pastors trying to get a point across and great for podcast sound bites, but they can feel frustrating for us when we're trying to actually put them into practice because we're not sure what they really mean. This week we're discussing one of the most popular: what it means to live "set apart."

Scattered throughout the Bible, God's call to set His children apart from the rest of the world is an important component of our mission here on Earth. But what does it really mean? How do we actually put it into practice?

I think we can find the answer in this portion of Philippians! As Paul's calling us to obedience like Jesus, he's teaching us the way of Jesus, a way that's different, *set apart,* from the world around us.

+ What's your understanding of what it means to be "set apart?" What questions do you have about it? Can you think of any Bible verses that talk about it?

Let's start here:

01 LIVE ON FIRE

+ FILL IN THE BLANKS BELOW FROM PHILIPPIANS 2:12-13.

"Therefore, my dear friends, as you have always obeyed—not only in my presence, but now much more in my absence—continue to __________ __________ your salvation with __________ and __________, for it is God who works in you to will and to act in order to fulfill his good purpose."

This is a juicy one! Paul's never been afraid of stepping on toes and he's certainly going for it here. After building his whole argument on the free gift of grace from Jesus, it almost seems like he's telling us our salvation requires work . . . What!?

Here's a Bible reading tip that's helped me in my journey through Scripture: It's important to always consider the context of the verses you're reading. To really understand what Paul's getting at here in verses 12 and 13, it helps to remember the audience he's writing to.

If you recall from Chapter 1 of our study, Paul started the church in Philippi years before he wrote this letter. He's writing to "dear friends" (v 12) who are, assumedly, *already saved.* So he's not writing to tell an unbeliever to earn their salvation by working. Instead, he's encouraging someone who's already received the gospel not to grow cold in their faith.

"... continue to work out your salvation ..."

I wonder if Paul had heard stories of Philippian believers who were on fire for Jesus when they first heard the Good News—ready to make any sacrifice, obey any command, and live as best they could in step with Christ's example—but had fallen off the wagon as the years had passed. They'd lost spiritual stamina and become people who called themselves Jesus followers but didn't have much proof of that belief leaking into their day to day lives.

This issue of spiritual complacency is addressed in lots of other places in Scripture, but we can find the most striking example in the book of Revelation.

"I know your deeds, that you are neither cold nor hot. I wish you were either one or the other! So, because you are lukewarm—neither hot nor cold—I am about to spit you out of my mouth."
Revelation 3:15-16 (emphasis added)

I bet you know some of these "lukewarm" Christians. It's your aunt who only goes to church on Easter and Christmas, your friend who goes to Bible study on a Thursday and the bars on a Friday, or the guy who leads worship at your church but cusses on His Instagram stories.

Honestly, if you think about it, maybe you'd describe yourself as lukewarm, too.

So many of us can relate to the believers in Philippi here. We need this message just as much as they did! I know there are so many areas of my own life that have gone cold. I find myself in conversations with an unbeliever at a coffee shop and I don't bring up Jesus, I zone out during worship at church, and I forget to pray more often than I remember to.

But here's the thing! We can't be "set apart" from everyone else if our salvation was a one-time thing. If we're more cold than hot in our faith, or a complacent kind of lukewarm, we end up just looking like the world, not making any moves for the Kingdom of God or growing closer to Jesus.

That's the danger Paul sees in these lukewarm Philippians as he tells them to "work out their salvation with fear and trembling." He knows that when we stop putting effort into our faith, numbness seeps in and becomes fertile ground for the enemy to have his way in dulling our light for the Lord. We need to be just as on fire as we were when first saved, ready to "work out" our salvation by growing in obedience to the Word, spiritual maturity, and communion with Christ.

+ Are there any areas of your life right now that feel "lukewarm?" What are they?

Luckily, Paul doesn't just leave us hanging after he calls us to live on fire for Jesus. He reminds us that Jesus is the one who gives us the fire in the first place!

"... for it is God who works in you to will and to act in order to fulfill his good purpose."
Philippians 2:13

It's the best news for you and I who often forget to "work out" our salvation. God, through His Spirit, offers us the power to live like Jesus.

+ What's one way you feel called to "work out" your salvation this week? (Ex: set a reminder on your phone to pray throughout the day, implement daily Bible study, challenge yourself to tell one person about Jesus each week, etc.)

We know to be set apart we need to be "hot" in our faith. So what's next? Let's continue on in our reading to find out.

+ FILL IN THE BLANKS BELOW FROM PHILIPPIANS 2:14-16.

"Do everything without grumbling or arguing, so that you may become ____________ and __________, "children of God without fault in a warped and crooked generation." Then you will ____________ among them like stars in the sky as you hold firmly to the word of life."

02 Be Holy

Last week we learned that we need Jesus, and that all of us are sinners who fall short of the glory of God. That knowledge can make reading Paul's call in verses 14-16 intimidating. But I don't want you to see words like "blameless" and "pure" and brush them off because they feel impossible! God's call to holiness is one of the best ways we can be set apart from the world around us and be beacons of light and hope for our friends who need Jesus.

The word Paul uses for "blameless" in Greek here is *amemptoi*,[1] meaning "above reproach." It doesn't mean sinless perfection. Instead, it's a further explanation of what it looks like to work out our salvation as believers! We're called to live in such a way that those who don't know Jesus can look at us and notice something's different about us. We do our best to stay blameless and pure because Jesus was and because it makes others curious about what makes us different.

If you think about it, holiness is one of the easiest ways to be a witness for Jesus when you're in college. It's easy because it's not very popular to be holy these days. Whether it's dressing modestly, waiting until you're married to have sex, choosing not to get drunk or cuss, practicing integrity with your school work . . . You might find yourself the only one in your sorority, your dorm floor, or your math class who's living like that. If that's not being set apart for Jesus, I don't know what is!

But, as easy as it is in theory, it's just as hard in practice. Holiness is hard when it's trendy to wear that revealing top. Holiness is hard when you're alone with that boy in the dark of your room at 11:00 o'clock a night. Holiness is hard when you get invited to the party, when you're angry, or when you're falling behind in chemistry.

But the promise here sounds worth the battle to me! Paul says that when we choose holiness, we will "shine among them like stars in the sky." (v 15) And, just like with the call against complacency, he doesn't just leave us hanging.

+ Look at Philippians 2:16 and underline "as you hold firmly to the word of life."

The knowledge of the gospel, what Paul refers to here as the "word of life," is our best ally in the fight for holiness. When we know how much Jesus loves us and how much He sacrificed for us and how much power He offers us through His Spirit, choosing small acts of holiness becomes a little bit easier every day until, one day, we realize we look a whole lot more like Jesus than we did two years ago, two months ago, or even two days ago.

THINK IT THROUGH

+ Do you know anyone who "shines" with holiness? Who is it? What makes them seem this way?

+ What parts of your life are blameless and pure? What parts do you struggle to keep holy?

I gotta say . . . I'm loving this lesson! Paul's words here are so tangible and practical for our lives as college women. And this last way we can be set apart might just be my favorite.

03 REJOICE

Read Philippians 2:17-18 and circle every time Paul says "rejoice."

NOTES:

My next door neighbor's name is Richard. He's an older guy who lives alone and he doesn't know the Lord. My husband and I often find ourselves chatting with him about our days, asking him about lawn care, or inviting him over for hot dogs. He hasn't yet said yes to our invitation for him to join us for church, but we're hopeful that day's coming.

The other day, we had a funny interaction with him. He's got this old car sitting in the corner of his driveway. I'm pretty sure it doesn't run and, to put it nicely, it's a little bit dusty. Apparently, someone had written a message in the dirt on the windshield:

Have a nice day!

Richard brought it up to my husband and I because he suspected that *I* was the one who had written it. I was, understandably, confused. I assured him I hadn't snuck onto his property to write an encouraging message on his car. I asked why he would think it was me who'd done it.

Well, because you're always so happy, he said. *It sounds like something you would say.*

It's a funny story, but I think it illustrates this last point for us. Richard barely knows me. All he's had are short conversations with me, most about the weather and a few where I've invited him to church. But what he remembers about me is my joy. What stands out about me to Richard is that I'm *happy.*

<u>What if what sets you apart the most is your joy?</u>

Paul wraps up his thoughts in chapter 2 by reminding his readers that he rejoices with them, even though he's in jail and is possibly about to be executed. And then he urges them to rejoice right along with him.

This kind of godly joy—a happiness that stands the test of trial, circumstance, and even a bad mood—is a neon sign pointing to your faith. Think of the happiest Christians you know! They don't necessarily have the easiest, most trouble-free lives. But they do have a joy so deep in Christ that it seeps out into everything they do.

It's the common theme all throughout the book of Philippians and the call for every believer: choose joy. Do you want to be different from the world who loves to whine and grumble? *Choose joy.* Do you want to be a beacon of hope to your friends who don't know the Lord? *Choose joy.*

It's simple yet profound. In light of the resurrection, we are armed with a supernatural joy that doesn't make sense, a soul-deep contentment that can't be rocked by the wind and waves of life. If Paul can rejoice in the midst of persecution, we can—through God's power—rejoice right where we are. Then maybe those around us will remember our "happy" vibes and wonder what makes us different. They'll wonder where that joy comes from.

NOTES:

+ Have you ever found yourself being a "grumpy Christian?" How can you choose joy this week?

Paul has painted an awesome picture for us of what it looks like to be set apart for Christ: to be women who are on fire, holy, and full of the joy of life with Jesus. So now I want to leave you with this.

Read Philippians 2:19-30.

We don't have time to dive too deeply into Paul's remarks about his friends Timothy and Epaphroditus, but I want you to notice the qualities he calls out in them. He describes Timothy as a man of unselfish love, work ethic, and servant heartedness. He applauds the courage of Epaphroditus. They are men who clearly "work out" their salvation in big ways.

What would you like to be written about you? What do you want to be remembered for?

Here's the encouragement we can all leave with: Today can be the day where we rely on God's power in a fresh way. Today, He can show us how to live like Jesus lived. He can help us to outgrow our complacency and become imbued with His joy and His holiness.

As a community, let's be remembered as women who "shine among [others] like stars in the sky as we hold firmly to the word of life."

PRAYERS & PRAISES

CONVERSATION

1. Paul encouraged the Philippians to continue obeying Jesus as they had before. What way of "working out your salvation" comes most naturally to you? (Scripture reading, prayer, service, worship, etc.) What are some works of faith you want to grow in?

2. What do you think makes it tough for us to stay holy as college women? What are some ways you can fight against that struggle in your day to day life?

3. Who do you know that is set apart by joy? How can you tangibly model this attitude in your own life?

4. Paul writes about Timothy and Epaphroditus as men who worked out their salvation in some awesome ways. What would you like to be written about you? How do you think others will remember your life and the way you lived for Jesus?

06

WHY AM I SO TIRED?

Why Am I So Tired?

PHILIPPIANS 3:1-11

I have to be real with you. I am *so* tired.

All in the past year, I struggled through a not-so-easy pregnancy, gave birth, and attempted to recover from pregnancy and birth while learning how to take care of a helpless little baby who doesn't believe in letting her parents sleep. Then, still exhausted and fresh to the whole parenthood thing, I went back to working full time. I'm trying to juggle everything and, honestly, I'm not not juggling very well.

But seriously, I am *trying so hard.*

I've always wanted other people to see me as a girl boss. I want to look capable and powerful, like I know what I'm doing and like I'm effortlessly good at everything I do. As silly as it sounds, I think I even want to trick God into thinking I have it all together. I want to earn His affection through my hustle. But in this season I'm watching things slip through the cracks left and right. I miss the mark trying to take care of my baby, I miss the mark trying to do my job well, and I can barely remember to feed myself.

Girl boss I am not.

All this makes me wonder . . . Is God as impressed by all my hard work as I think He is? Has He fallen for my attempts at keeping up appearances?

Am I more godly now because I've pulled myself up by my bootstraps?

You're probably not in the same season of life as I am right now, but I'm thinking you may be able to relate to this try-hard attitude I'm stuck in.

You busted your butt to get into your dream school on scholarship, but now you're watching as your grades are slipping even though you study 'til 2 AM every day.

You joined that club to find friends, but now you're struggling to keep up the friendly facade as you slowly become overwhelmed with coffee dates, events, parties, and surface level conversations.

You met that boy when you were feeling on top of the world, but now you're in a valley season struggling to live up to the girl he expects you to be, fighting tooth and nail to save the relationship from going under.

You fill in the blank. We're all striving for something and judging ourselves with sky-high standards we can never live up to. But aren't you *tired* of living like this? I certainly am!

I believe God has a solution for the try-hard, striving-for-perfection mindset we find ourselves stuck in. He has a better way for our lives that won't leave us so burnt out and soul-deep sleepy.

Let's dive back into our study of the book of Philippians to find what that solution is.

STOP & PRAY

LORD, I SURRENDER MY STRIVING TO YOU AND I ASK FOR YOUR REST. REALIGN MY PRIORITIES WITH YOURS AND REVEAL YOUR HEART FOR ME THROUGH YOUR WORD.

Read Philippians 3:1-11.

+ Go ahead and draw your own conclusions about this week's reading. Which verses stand out to you? What do you think is Paul's main message in this section of Philippians?

As usual, we're going to need to grab some context before we can really understand Paul's message here. If you started reading and got tripped up by "dogs" and "circumcision," don't worry! You're not alone, it's strange wording for our modern brains.

Essentially, Paul is writing in response to a group of Jews-turned-Jesus-followers called the "Circumcision Party" or the "Judaizers." They believed that if you were a non-Jewish person (Gentile) who converted to the Christian faith, you needed to be circumcised to be welcomed into the fold; to be clean in God's eyes and acceptable in their eyes. This really fired Paul up because they were diminishing the power of the gospel by adding qualifications to it. Suddenly, instead of being saved by faith in Jesus through His work on the cross and *only* through Jesus, now you had to jump through Jewish hoops as well.[1]

Obviously, that's a big no no because that's just not what the gospel is at all.

Paul was so riled up he called them "dogs." It's the same insult these Judaizers would have used against the Gentiles, calling them as unclean as a dog roaming the streets with fleas and rummaging through people's trash.

So, by turning that insult right back at them, Paul made it clear that he does not stand with the Circumcision Party.

And it's within his defense of the simple gospel where we find the first tidbit we want to focus in on for our study this week. Check it out!

> *"For it is we who are the circumcision, we who serve God by his Spirit, who boast in Christ Jesus, and who put no confidence in the flesh . . ."*
> *Philippians 3:3 (emphasis added)*

According to Paul, "we" who have received salvation through faith in Christ Jesus don't put our confidence in the flesh. But I'm already seeing a problem here because, like I said, *I put my confidence in the flesh all the time.*

01 PUT NO CONFIDENCE IN THE FLESH

Let's give a definition for "flesh" real quick before we really flesh out the meaning of these verses. (Did you laugh at my pun? No? OK, let's ignore it and keep moving.)

"The flesh describes the values and activities of humanity unaided by the Holy Spirit."[2]

NOTES:

Paul goes on in the next few verses to describe his fleshly accomplishments and achievements that he used to think were impressive, but now recognizes as empty striving without the Spirit of God.

+ Look back at Philippians 3:4-6 and jot down some of Paul's accomplishments.

If we get super honest with ourselves, we all have lists like that. It's the things we think make us good in the eyes of others or even good in the eyes of God. While Paul says he was a zealous Jew faultless in the law, we say we go to church every Sunday, we serve in a soup kitchen, we have the top grades in our class, we've never smoked . . . The list goes on.

Our accolades, achievements, skillsets, and even good works become fleshly idols when we use them as ways to look good before the Lord or to look good before others. Paul knew this intimately, as we can tell by his very next words.

+ FILL IN THE BLANKS BELOW FROM PHILIPPIANS 3:7.

"But whatever were ____________ to me I now consider ____________ for the sake of Christ."

Remember how tired you are? Remember how empty all those accolades make you feel in the end? Remember how burnt out you get trying to always do the right thing in your own power?

It's a *loss.*

And I think God made us this way. It's a gift of His grace that the things we run to could never fill us, just as the Judaizers couldn't save themselves through circumcision. When we realize we've been chasing the flesh, our eyes naturally turn to Jesus, the only one who can fill that tired, striving, legalistic hole in our hearts.

When we realize we're lost, we know how much we stand to gain in the merciful hands of our Savior.

+ Do you have your own list of fleshly accomplishments like Paul's? Write it out below.

All this begs the question . . . If we're not supposed to put our confidence in the flesh, what do we put our confidence in? According to Paul, it's the very Person our fleshly "loss" turns our eyes to.

02 The Surpassing Worth of Christ

Reread Philippians 3:7-9.

This might sound weird, but I think I can empathize with the Circumcision Party. It must have felt nice to have a physical marker for salvation, a line in the sand they could draw and say, *I've earned my place with God! I'm good! I'm going to Heaven!*

Because isn't that what we're doing when we strive for God's approval? We're trying to find a "thing" that's worth more to God than what Jesus did on the cross. We're so uncomfortable with the free gift of grace that we want to add a caveat to it, just in case God really wanted our good works as an entry ticket to Heaven all along.

But here's what Paul has to say against that mindset we get stuck in: There is *nothing* worth more than Jesus.

"... I consider everything a loss because of the surpassing worth of knowing Christ Jesus my Lord... I consider them garbage, that I may gain Christ and be found in him, not having a righteousness of my own that comes from the law, but that which is through faith in Christ..."
Philippians 3:8-9

Because he's so sure of the worth of Jesus's salvation, Paul is giving up his try-hard attitude and his striving for accomplishment. It's the biggest leap we perfectionists can take, betting it all on what Jesus did for us instead of what we can do for Him.

I'm fascinated by the word Paul uses for our fleshly works here in verse 8. *Garbage.* Written *sybalon* in the Greek, it's a word that might even mean *dung*. Is Paul really saying that all our good works—that my attempts at looking like a girl boss after having my first baby—are really just poop in God's eyes?

I hate to break it to you, sister, as much as I hate to break it to myself but . . . the answer is yes.

+ FIND ISAIAH 64:6 IN YOUR BIBLE AND FILL IN THE BLANKS BELOW.

"All of us have become like one who is unclean, and all our ______________ ______________ are like ______________ ______________; we all shrivel up like a leaf, and like the wind our sins sweep us away."

As hard as you try, your righteous acts are nothing but filthy rags in comparison to the perfection and glory of Jesus. And once we embrace that truth, really and truly, it has the potential to lift that heavy weight of striving off our back.

I can stop trying to be enough because it will never work. Jesus is already more than enough for me.

THINK IT THROUGH

+ Get super honest . . . Have you ever found yourself forgetting the "worth" of what Jesus did for you on the cross? What season of your life, thing, or event caused you to feel this way?

+ Brainstorm! Next time you forget the worth of Jesus's work on the cross and find yourself placing confidence in your flesh, how do you want to remind yourself of what He did for you? Jot down some ideas below! (Ex: meditating on a specific Bible verse, confiding in a sister in Christ, singing a specific worship song, etc.)

NOTES:

Wow! This Scripture has called us out and called us higher in the best way! Let's look back at the last two verses as we wrap up this week's teaching.

+ Copy down Philippians 3:10-11 in the space below.

03 KNOW HIM

It would be a little silly to assume that, in a few pages of a book, we've managed to fully answer the question, *"Why am I so tired?"* I think, unfortunately, that's a question we're going to be facing for the rest of our lives, and there are certainly things other than striving that can cause us to feel spiritually worn out. But, I do believe Paul's writing in this portion of Philippians has taught us where to set our eyes when that exhaustion from striving starts to set in. After toiling for so long with our stare set on our own accomplishments (on our flesh) we're reminded to look to Jesus, the one who paid it all with His body on the cross and paid for our sins in full.

Instead of setting another goal for ourself that we'll inevitably fall short of, we can adopt the simple plea of Paul's heart we find in verse 10:

I want to know Christ.

This was what years of the whittling down of his legalistic faith brought him to. He who started as a pious, zealous, prideful, and blinded Jew was now a man who simply wanted to know His Savior. It's a desire impossible for the legalist, who is forced to focus on her own performance and status to find some kind of peace with God. But Paul wanted Jesus, not himself; Jesus's performance, not His own.[3]

What if instead of trying to be the best first-time mom there ever was and blow everyone out of the water with my capability, I could just know Jesus as my provider in the 2AM wake up calls?

What if instead of beating yourself up about your grades and constantly feeling like you're letting yourself down, you could just know Jesus as the One who loves you, even when you feel like you haven't earned it?

What if instead of trying desperately to be the perfect Christian, the perfect girlfriend, the perfect daughter, or the perfect friend, you could just know Jesus as the One who was perfect so you don't have to be?

+ What area of your life do you need to trade striving for knowing Jesus?

OK, OK. I hear you! *I get that I shouldn't strive for God's approval. I get that God doesn't want me to feel so exhausted and burnt out. But what about working out my salvation? What about doing good things? What about growing in my faith?*

This is the kicker! God does not desire for us to sit on our booties while the world passes us by, falling into laziness because some girl in a Bible study told us to stop trying so hard! His Word still commands us to prove our faith with our actions (James 2:18), to do the good works we were created for (Ephesians 2:10), to go and make disciples (Matthew 28:19), and to let our lights shine for the world to see (Matthew 5:16). But it's the *heart* from which we do these things that matters!

KEEP GROWING

WE LISTED FOUR VERSES ABOVE THAT TALK ABOUT GOD'S CALL TO ACTION FOR OUR LIVES (JAMES 2:18, EPHESIANS 2:10, MATTHEW 28:19, MATTHEW 5:16). IN YOUR OWN TIME, LOOK THESE VERSES UP AND STUDY THEM. CAN YOU FIND ANY OTHER VERSES ABOUT GOD'S CALL ON OUR LIVES AS JESUS FOLLOWERS?

When we start with knowing Jesus, we are energized, empowered, and guided to go do all the wonderful, world-shaking things that He's called us to do! And Paul recognized this, too! Look back at verse 10:

"...yes, to know the power of His resurrection..."

Does that wording ring a bell? Paul wrote about this resurrection power in his letter to the Ephesians!

"I pray that the eyes of your heart may be enlightened in order that you may know the hope to which he has called you, the riches of his glorious inheritance in his holy people, and his incomparably great power for us who believe. That power is the same as the mighty strength he exerted when he raised Christ from the dead and seated him at his right hand in the heavenly realms,"
Ephesians 1:18-20 (emphasis added)

The same power that raised Christ from the dead lives in you. It's not a power you have to earn. It's a power freely gifted to you by Jesus and, when you know Him—when you really, truly know Him—it's a power that flows in and through you to make not only you, but also the people around you look a little more like Jesus every day.

Are you tired? Maybe it's a sign that you've been operating apart from the Spirit of God. You've been working too hard on too many things that don't matter to Jesus. Accept His invitation today to count it all as loss and gain the greatest gift: *Him.*

Sister, the solution to the struggle is a lot simpler than we've made it seem. Look to Jesus, the author and perfecter of your faith. In Him, you will find rest for your soul.

PRAYERS & PRAISES

CONVERSATION

1. Are you feeling burnt out or tired right now? What do you think is the cause?

2. What 'work of the flesh' do you find hardest to count as loss? Why do you think that is?

3. Think back to when you first gave your life to Jesus. Do you feel like you know Him better now than you did then? How do you think your relationship has grown since it first began?

4. We can stop striving to be enough for Jesus because He is already enough for us. Look back at the practical step to fighting a heart of striving you wrote about in the Think It Through section. What's your plan for implementing that practice this week?

07

WHAT ABOUT MY PAST?

WHAT ABOUT MY PAST?

PHILIPPIANS 3:12-14

We've got a lot to talk about this week ladies, so let's go ahead and jump in.

Read Philippians 3:12-14.

This portion of Scripture wraps up Paul's thought process from the last chapter of our study. As we've come to expect from him, he keeps it humble by reminding his readers that even he hasn't "arrived" at this goal of spiritual maturity he's been describing. Then, he throws in a "but" that precedes some of the most powerful and difficult verses we've read yet.

+ FILL IN THE BLANKS BELOW FROM PHILIPPIANS 3:12.

"Not that I have already obtained all this, or have already arrived at my goal, __________ __________ __________ __________ to take hold of that for which Christ Jesus took hold of me."

But I press on.

It's a phrase used throughout the New Testament, but the translation from the Greek varies slightly depending on the context. It's translated as "press on" here, but in other parts of Scripture it's translated as "make every effort, strive, follow, run after, hunt down, or pursue." Paul's telling his readers that he is committed to continuing the fight. He's straining toward what's ahead (v 13). Remember, in the context of these verses, "what's ahead" is his goal to become more like Jesus.

We all have some sort of desire within us to "press on." If you've made it this far in this study, I think it's safe to say you're committed to pursuing and making every effort to grow in your faith. But that desire is constantly impeded within our hearts by continuing's worst enemy: *our past.*

> *"... Forgetting what is behind and straining toward what is ahead, I press on..."*
> *Philippians 3:13b-14a (emphasis added)*

My husband loves to run. Specifically, he loves to run marathons. Not a runner myself, I'm always amazed by his dedication and athleticism. I cried just as hard at the finish line of his fifth marathon as I did at his first. My proximity to the marathon lifestyle has me considering the process of spiritual growth in a similar way.

Pressing on is a lot like running a marathon. We set out on a long journey knowing there will be hard moments, knowing we will need to refuel along the way, knowing we may get an hour of runner's high or a leg cramp, and knowing the strength instilled in us through long months of preparation is what we'll lean on.

Now, imagine someone tied a rope around your waist at the starting line and attached a 300 pound rock to the end of it. Then, boom, the starting whistle sounds and you're expected to run. Sounds a lot harder, right?

Our past is that rock tied around us. As great as our intentions are to press on and run the race set before us in a heavenward direction (v 14), we are consistently held back by the things we did in our past we're ashamed of, the things done to us we can't let go of, and the toxic narratives we keep repeating to ourselves over and over.

Here's my goal this week: that we can untie the rope. Through the power of the Holy Spirit, we can "forget what is behind," as Paul says, and run confidently in the direction God's calling us.

STOP & PRAY

GOD, THANK YOU FOR YOUR FORGIVENESS. SHOW ME HOW TO FORGET MY PAST AND PRESS ON TOWARD YOUR HEAVENLY CALL.

So, *what about my past?*

Paul's actually the best guy to answer this question because his past is pretty nasty. We've alluded to it off and on throughout our study, but let's take some time to read Paul's conversion story before we continue.

01 WE ALL HAVE A PAST

Read Acts 9:1-22.

+ In your own words, summarize Paul's conversion story below.

Paul (formerly referred to as Saul) was a major hater of the early Jesus followers. He wasn't just leaving mean comments on their Instagram posts . . . this man was actively seeking out Christians to have them imprisoned and killed. It's not exactly the best backstory for your favorite preacher to have. But, in a crazy cool miracle story, Saul/Paul encountered Jesus on his way to continue persecuting Christians, and his whole life was drastically and dramatically changed.

Here's what I want us to pay attention to:

+ FILL IN THE BLANKS BELOW FROM ACTS 9:20.

"____________ ____________ he began to preach in the synagogues that Jesus is the Son of God."

In just the span of a few days, Paul went from infamous Christian-killer to *at once* beginning to preach that Jesus is God. The story continues by saying that the people of Damascus were "astonished" and "baffled" and, yeah, I get it!

I think most of us would have taken a little bit of time to lie low and let people forget about our indiscretions before we showed up with a personality transplant. But Paul didn't let who he used to be define who God had changed him into. *At once* he dropped his old self and stepped into his new identity in Christ.

You could say it this way: Paul forgot what was behind and pressed on toward what was ahead.

But this is what we've got to face! It's hard to do that. If we're being real, all of us have a past. All of us have something heavy enough to weigh us down when we're trying to run the race with God. Yours might not be as dramatic as Paul's, but I can guarantee it's there.

You slept with so many guys before you met Jesus that you feel like you can't tell the girl you're discipling that she shouldn't do that weekend getaway with her boyfriend.

You posted all of those Snapchat stories smoking and drinking at freshman year parties and now you can't stomach posting a Bible verse because, what would people think?

You want to ask that friend to stop gossiping about your mutual acquaintance, but just last week you were the one leading the convo about how much she annoys you.

THINK IT THROUGH

+ Consider . . . What part of your past feels heaviest these days?

+ What "change" might that part of your past be holding you back from?

God is great at changing everything for us in an instant. But we aren't so great at moving on from what we were freed from. So how did Paul so quickly—and seemingly effortlessly—go from persecutor to preacher? What's the secret? *What about my past?!*

It's God. He's the key to dropping the past and the key to pressing on. Paul didn't do it in his own power and neither can we.

02 GOD FORGIVES AND FORGETS

We often accidentally find ourselves reading the Bible as though it's about us when it's really all about God. And I think it's possible (and dangerous) for us to do that when reading these verses from Philippians. Yes, Paul says that he presses on, he forgets what is behind, and he strains ahead, but that's just one side of the story. And honestly, it's the less important part of the story.

+ Look back at Philippians 3:12-14 and underline every time Paul mentions God. (Hint: Jesus is God, too!)

Paul presses on because Christ Jesus took hold of him. He presses on toward the calling God gave him. He's running, yes, but He's chasing Jesus to Heaven through God's power.

This is what we need to remember as we seek to do the same. Yes, it's hard for us to forget our past. But, it's actually really easy for God.

Read Psalm 103:8-12.

+ What do these verses teach you about God?

While it's my character to hold onto my past, to harbor shame for my mistakes, and to withhold forgiveness, it's God's character to love without anger. It's God's character to throw my past away, as far as the east is from the west. It's God's character to treat me better than I deserve. Our good God *chooses* to remember your sins no more (Isaiah 43:25).

And with our salvation in Jesus, that characteristic of God is even more apparent.

"Therefore, if anyone is in Christ, the new creation has come: The old has gone, the new is here!"
2 Corinthians 5:17

NOTES:

Jesus died so that you could receive forgiveness for your sins. Jesus died so that you could stand before God with a clean slate. Jesus died so that you wouldn't have to hold onto the things you're holding on to.

So why are we still holding them?

The Bible says that if we confess our sins, God will forgive us (1 John 1:9). Maybe we keep holding onto the shame of our past because we forget how simple it is to give it to God. Sister, you're not better at sinning than God is at forgiving. You're not better at remembering than He is at forgetting. The freedom you've been desperate for could be as simple as a conversation with your Maker, a conversation that could sound something like this . . .

God, I'm so embarrassed by who I used to be. I'm sorry for those decisions I made. Will you forgive me and let me walk in freedom?

God, I'm stuck in this shame. Could you remind me of your character? What does it mean that you forget my past?

God, I can't forgive myself for the things I've done and I can't forget the things that have been done to me. Will you remind me of your abounding love?

+ Let's have a conversation with God. Journal your prayers, thoughts, questions, and confessions below. (Want help getting started? Try praying the words of Psalm 34:5!)

Relying on the goodness of God and claiming His forgiveness over the worst parts of you is the supernatural way of forgetting what's behind. It's the way you sever your ties with the weight of your past. And once that past is severed—whether it's one time or a lifetime of daily help from the Lord for the forgetting process—you can run in full confidence toward the calling God has placed on your life.

03 We're Running Toward Heaven

Isn't it crazy that we've been studying just three verses from Scripture and we've had this much to talk about? This is why I'm obsessed with God's Word! We could meditate on these short sentences for years and still be learning new things about our Creator!

For now, let's focus on the last few words as we land the plane for this chapter.

+ Copy Philippians 3:14 in the space below.

How often do we get so caught up in the past that we forget the *prize* God has ahead of us? Maybe that's why the enemy loves for us to dwell on our mistakes or the tragedies we've walked through. He knows if he can get us distracted and off balance by things God calls us to forget, we won't be able to run toward the wonderful things God has in store for our future.

+ Look back at the verse above and circle "prize."

This isn't the only time Paul mentions a prize in his writings to the early church. He, just like my pastor, loves a good sports analogy.

"Do you not know that in a race all the runners run, but only one gets the prize? Run in such a way as to get the prize. Everyone who competes in the games goes into strict training. They do it to get a crown that will not last, but we do it to get a crown that will last forever."
1 Corinthians 9:24-25 (emphasis added)

The prize he's referring to here is no secret. Jesus calls us heavenward, remember? The prize and crown awaiting every single believer is an eternal life in God's presence; forever in Heaven with no pain, tears, or darkness. And really, that's enough to make me want to drop my past like a hot potato! I don't want to try to take that heavy rock with me to Heaven!

But, God is so good that He also gives us little prizes along the way. He loves to pepper our lives with sweet prizes, gifts we could never have earned for ourselves and "wins" that we did nothing to deserve. What if God's got something better for you on the other side of forgiveness?

Paul is a great example of this. If he had stayed trapped in his shame and weighed down by his past and chosen not to receive God's forgiveness for his life, he would have missed out on so much fruit God wanted to grow in him and through him. Persecutor Saul turned into Evangelist, Church Planter, Preacher, and Discipler Paul who wrote most of our New Testament, started many first century churches, performed miracles, and won Gentiles for Christ.

God didn't just redeem Paul and leave him there! He redeemed Paul and then poured His Spirit out into the world through him.

KEEP GROWING

THE BIBLE IS FULL OF REDEMPTION STORIES JUST LIKE PAUL'S. SPEND SOME TIME THIS WEEK DIGGING THROUGH THE WORD AND FINDING SOME! (WE'D RECOMMEND STARTING WITH RUTH, JOB, AND HANNAH!)

NOTES:

God doesn't promise us an easy life. (Remember, Paul was shipwrecked multiple times, spent a lot of time in jail, and ultimately died a martyr for his faith.) You will have hard times ahead of you no matter who you are! But we can't let our hangups on the past cause us to fear the future. I believe God has good things in store for your earthly life and little prizes to plant in and through you. But even if He didn't, you are still promised the eternal prize of Heaven! That's the finish line we set our eyes to as we press on. *We forget what's behind and we run toward Heaven.*

+ Do you ever find yourself fearing the future? Why do you think that is?

In the seventh grade, I had a little cussing problem. OK, maybe not a *little* cussing problem. It was a big one. It was so bad that (true story) a girl named Hadley was told by her mom to move lunch tables because I was a bad influence.

Now, the Lord has freed me from my cussing problems (Hallelujah!). But, I think about that season of my life–and Hadley–often. I imagine what it would be like if I ran into her today. Would she be shocked by the way I've changed? Would I feel embarrassed about my history with her? What if I tried to share the gospel with her? Would she be able to see past my old bad behavior?

But those are the thoughts the enemy wants me to think. He wants me to spiral in my head about my past. He wants me to forget how powerful it is that God has redeemed me. Because the reality is, it's a *good* thing that Hadley would be shocked by who I am now! It's a *good* thing that I'm unrecognizable from who I used to be.

NOTES:

The past me is a testimony that God can change everything.

Yes, you might have some things in your past you aren't proud of. We all do! But they don't disqualify you from the race; they're proof of the wonder of God's forgiveness and His grace. You are evidence of the redemptive power of Jesus's work on the cross!

Growing in Christ is a marathon. *But you aren't tied down*. You are held tight by the Holy Spirit of God who is redeeming you and drawing you to the finish line.

"I forget all of the past as I fasten my heart to the future instead."
Philippians 2:14, The Passion Translation

PRAYERS & PRAISES

CONVERSATION

1. Let's get super honest. What's the rock tied around you that keeps you from running the race God has set before you?

2. When you think about your past, what kind of feelings come up? (shame, embarrassment, guilt, confusion, sadness, pride, joy, etc.)

3. What advice or wisdom would you share with the younger version of yourself who was weighed down in sin or shame? How can you receive that wisdom today?

4. 2 Corinthians 5:17 says that the old is gone and the new is here! Take a moment and dream with God . . . What does the 'new you' look like?

08

WHO SHOULD I FOLLOW?

WHO SHOULD I FOLLOW?

PHILIPPIANS 3:15-21

Confession: I'm not very hip with the trends. As millennial as it sounds, I see the popular TikTok trends two weeks late when they cycle over to Instagram reels and I have to text my Gen-Z sister for explanations when new "lingo" hits the internet.

That lack of coolness had me shocked a few years ago when I overheard some girls at a coffee shop gossiping about one of their friends. The insult they chose was wild to me: *Have you seen her For You Page? So embarrassing!*

I guess you can tell a lot about a person based on what the social media algorithm cooks up to show them. For example, my husband's Instagram only suggests dog videos to him. You can't really hide what content you're consuming at 3AM because the little robot in your phone will bring it right back up for you at 11AM in the hallway between classes.

These are modern problems we're facing, issues we'd assume the Bible doesn't cover because they didn't even have flip phones yet. But fortunately, the Bible doesn't even have to try to stay relevant—it just is.

KEEP GROWING

ISAIAH 40:8 SAYS THAT, "THE GRASS WITHERS AND THE FLOWERS FALL, BUT THE WORD OF OUR LORD ENDURES FOREVER." WHY DO YOU THINK THE BIBLE HAS BEEN ABLE TO ENDURE IN A WAY NOTHING ELSE CAN? CAN YOU FIND ANY OTHER BIBLE VERSES ABOUT THE POWER OF THE WORD OF GOD?

As crazy as it might sound, I believe Paul has an answer for our FYP problems in the next portion of Philippians. God's going to address our hearts this week as we address this question: *Who should I follow?* Whether on social media or in real life, we're all following somebody who follows somebody else, and unless Jesus is the one leading, the end of the road isn't somewhere you'll want to be.

STOP & PRAY

LORD, I WANT YOU AND ONLY YOU. I SURRENDER THE THINGS I'VE SET MY EYES ON THAT AREN'T OF YOU AND I ASK THAT YOU WOULD DIRECT MY VISION IN THE RIGHT DIRECTION.

OK, I know you're so ready to jump back into the Word so let's do it!

Read Philippians 3:15-21.

+ What stands out to you from the Scripture on the last page?

Already in verse 15 Paul stays true to his slightly-savage self, simultaneously calling us out and calling us higher.

"All of us, then, who are mature should take such a view of things. And if on some point you think differently, that too God will make clear to you."
Philippians 3:15

Wrapping up the entirety of chapter 3, Paul's calling us to be mature believers (remember, the whole point of this study!), then he's politely telling us to mind our own business and stop fighting in the comment section.

Verse 17 gives us the meat of our conversation this week.

+ FILL IN THE BLANKS BELOW FROM PHILIPPIANS 3:17.

"Join ________ in ________ my example, brothers and sisters, and just as you have us as a model, keep your ________ on those who live as we do."

As Christians, we are called to join together in following those who follow Jesus; setting our eyes on older, wiser, and more mature disciples of Christ as we seek to become just as solid in our faith walks. "Follow my example, as I follow the example of Christ," Paul writes in one of his other church letters (1 Corinthians 11:1). But I think, if we're being honest, that directive can get a little difficult in this day and age.

01 FOLLOW THOSE WHO FOLLOW JESUS

Let's think again about the setting in which Paul is writing. Remember, Jesus had just died, resurrected, and ascended into Heaven. His command to "make disciples of all nations" had just hit the scene. Though the church in Philippi was one of the more established Jesus communities of the time, everyone was still what we could consider as "baby Christians." (In fact, the name "Christian" hadn't even become popularized yet!)

So, it's significant that after spending three chapters giving the Philippians great advice for how to live like Christ, Paul encourages them to join together and follow the example of Christians who are following Jesus even more confidently. I think there's a lesson hidden in there: As much as hearing what to do and learning what's right is important, the best way to activate that godly goodness into our lives is to do it within the context of community.

Translation: We are called to follow those who follow Jesus.

One of the most popular contexts we see this put into action is through *discipleship*. This is when you find an older and wiser person in your church or your Bible study who you respect and you hang around them and learn from them as they live their lives chasing after Jesus. The more you spend time with them, the more you'll find yourself living like they live and, hopefully, the more like Jesus you will become.

But I don't think any of us object to the idea of discipleship! I *love* having mentors and disciplers to spend time with. I have no issue modeling my life after theirs or letting them teach me new things. Following them is a no-brainer.

But, when it comes to social media, who we follow feels a little bit murkier. We've become experts at separating our church life from our online life. Sure, we're smart and discerning when choosing a church mentor, but we let just about anybody disciple us online. The danger is, the same process happens on our TikTok accounts as it does in our lives. The more time we spend watching that influencer, the more we start to agree with them, and the more we start to act like them. *But if that person isn't following Jesus, we are in trouble of being made into their image instead of His.*

The truth is, these things are shaping us whether we intend for them to or not. So, if we don't take action in filtering the influences that we come across, the cost to our hearts could be astronomical.

> *"Above all else, guard your heart, for everything you do flows from it."*
> *Proverbs 4:23*

Now, I'm not here to condemn you for who you follow. I'm not telling you to throw your phone away and start living off-grid. But, I do want to challenge you to be as discerning as you can with who you follow. Evaluate: Is consuming this person's content making me more like Jesus? If not, it may be time to make some changes!

Here's a trick of the trade. Use the Bible to help you figure out if someone is a good "discipler" (whether online or in person) . . .

★ JOHN 13:34-35 COMMANDS US TO LOVE ONE ANOTHER AS CHRIST LOVED US.

Does this person love others well?

★ JOHN 15:16 TELLS US TO BEAR FRUIT.

Does this person showcase the fruit of the Spirit in their lives?

★ JOHN 8:31 CALLS US TO ABIDE IN THE WORD.

Do I feel confident that this person spends time in the Word of God?

THINK IT THROUGH

+ Consider . . . Who do you follow (in person or online) that makes you more like Jesus? Who do you follow that does not?

+ We use the word of God to help us find good people to follow. Can you find any other godly qualities in Scripture you want to keep in mind when considering someone to disciple you?

NOTES:

We have to be careful not to allow ourselves to be discipled by anyone and everyone. Because, as we'll see as our study of Philippians continues, that can be a slippery slope.

Read Philippians 3:18-19.

It's a truth so heartbreaking it brought Paul to tears . . .

"... many live as enemies of the cross of Christ."
Philippians 3:18b

But if I'm being real with you, my first response to the "enemies of the cross" isn't usually to cry for them as Paul does. I respond with apathy, preferring to hang with my Christian friends and pretend those other people don't exist. I respond with anger, especially when those enemies commit great injustices. And sometimes, I even respond with jealousy, wondering why God's right way of living can seem so boring compared to their way (or at least the way they portray it online).

As much as we are called to shield our eyes and protect our hearts from influences that may try to lead us away from God's best for us, we cannot forget that there are those all around us whose "destiny is destruction." And the only way that destiny can change is through God's power and our invitation.

02 Be Someone Worth Following

Let's revisit that marathon metaphor from last week. Imagine you're confidently running the race and all the sudden, you see someone running in the wrong direction. What would you do? Let them keep running? Or, would you grab them by the arm, turn them around, and show them the right direction to run to finish the race?

As followers of Jesus, we are called to be the one who stops and offers aid to the wayward runner. When we've found someone to follow as *they* follow Jesus, we are equipped and empowered to allow someone to follow us as *we* follow Jesus. It's the cycle of discipleship!

But, that beautiful circle of invitation and mentorship often gets caught up somewhere in the middle, for lots of different reasons. Maybe you're still hung up on who you're following and finding someone to follow you feels like a big step. Maybe you don't really care about the person who's wayward and you're still asking God for a tender heart toward them. Or, maybe the way you're living out your Christian life isn't really worth following.

Oof. It's a gut punch! But, as hard as it is to consider, all of us have been there at one time or another! We've all run the squiggly line instead of the straight one and we've all presented a blurry image of Christ for the people around us. There's no condemnation here! But, there is a really cool invitation for us to be strong runners who can grab any gal who's struggling and bring her with us to the finish line.

> *"In the same way, let your light shine before others, that they may see your good deeds and glorify your Father in heaven."*
> *Matthew 5:16*

Think again about your social media accounts. Are you presenting a confusing image of Christ for someone seeking faith? When we have a Bible verse in our bio but revealing pictures in our feed, *it hurts our witness.* When we post a story at church in the morning then at a party getting drunk at night, *it hurts our witness.* Or, if we never post about our faith at all, *it hurts our witness.*

In the same way that you can get accidentally discipled by those you follow online, you are also discipling those who stumble across whatever content you're putting out there. This is such a unique opportunity! Paul had to endure three shipwrecks and days-long walks in the hot sun to tell a new person about Jesus. You can do it with three clicks on your phone! But, if we waste this opportunity or use it carelessly, we're allowing the ones Jesus loves to keep running confidently in the wrong direction, a direction that leads to destruction.

+ Evaluate the current state of your social media accounts. Is it obvious to someone seeing your feed that you're a Christian? Why or why not? (If you're not on social media, consider the same question for your day to day life!)

NOTES:

When we know that our citizenship is in Heaven (v 20), it's natural to want to bring as many people with us to that glorious finish line as we can. But, I wonder if there are some of you reading this who are starting to feel a little bit . . . overwhelmed. You're considering how to find someone to disciple you, how to do an audit of who you're following on social media, how to be a light and evangelist online, and how to live out your faith in an outward and obvious way. And all of that is starting to feel like an impossible pressure, one that makes you want to just throw away your phone and go back to bed.

Here's the good news, sister:
Read Philippians 3:20-21.

03 TRANSFORMATION IS IN GOD'S HANDS

Something about these final two verses of Philippians 3 always grabs my attention. It just feels so quintessentially Paul. You can almost hear his voice as he's encouraging his friends . . . *Remember, guys! Jesus is coming back! And He's gonna make everything new! Set your eyes toward Heaven!*

That same encouragement goes for us, too. To the girl struggling with who to follow and how to be someone worth following, the message is the very same: Jesus is coming back, your home is in Heaven, and God is full of transforming power.

Can you think all the way back to Chapter 1 of our study? (Take some time to flip back there if you need a refresher real quick!) God, in His endless grace, gives us *room to grow*. He's not sitting up in Heaven ready to condemn you because you follow that influencer or because you reposted that video last week. He loves you so much that He's willing to be in it with you for the long haul. He wants to do the hard work of transformation in your life step by step.

He wants to run the race right alongside you.

I feel the struggle of slow transformation so acutely in my own life. Because of my age and the fun ministry position I get to hold, I find myself getting asked by younger women if I would disciple them more often than you would expect. One of those precious girls is Alexa, a friend I've been sharing my life with for over three years now.

Three years ago, when she was a sophomore in college and I was a high-energy twenty-something who hadn't yet gone through infertility, a tragic loss, or stepped into motherhood, I felt like I had a lot to offer her. We would meet up and discuss theology, go through a Bible study, or read a book together. We always had another coffee date on the calendar and our time never felt wasted.

But then, over the years as she got smarter and I got more tired, I started to feel like I had nothing for her. We'd go weeks without meeting and then, when I could finally find time to invite her over, she was greeted with a messy house and a messy me. I'd cry to her about my life as I tried to tell her how God was working in my heart, and I'd tell her I didn't know the answers to the bigger questions she'd started to ask. I felt like the blossoming spiritual maturity I had seen in her was not present in me, like the student was very quickly surpassing the teacher.

Then, when she experienced a tragic loss in her own life, I saw God's grace as she used what I had thought were wasted hours talking in circles to navigate her own grief in a similar way to how I had navigated mine. I saw God's grace when she got married and took little bits of what she'd witnessed of my marriage in those hectic days at my house and put them into practice in her own marriage. I saw God's grace when she started a new job and remembered little things I had told her years before and applied them to this new challenge.

God used me—someone not worth following in so many moments—to impact Alexa, a daughter He treasures. *He's just that good!*

If you're waiting to be a fully transformed, perfect person to have an impact on someone else, you'll be waiting forever. Even Paul was imperfect! He always wrote about his inadequacies, even referring to a "thorn" in his flesh he could never quite get rid of (2 Corinthians 12:7). Yet still, in his imperfection, he said . . .

"Join together in following my example, brothers and sisters . . . "
Philippians 3:17

NOTES:

So if you feel like you're unequipped to equip others or if you are frustrated with your slow progress as you are transformed into the image of Christ, then you're in good company. You are worth following because you follow the One who is able to "bring everything under his control" (v 21). He's not going to let you down!

Here's my best tip for how to transform within the context of community: Memorize this Bible verse.

"But he said to me, 'My grace is sufficient for you, for my power is made perfect in weakness.'"
2 Corinthians 12:9

Within the sufficiency of God's grace and an awareness of our own endless weaknesses, there is so much room for growth. We are then enabled to give our friend grace when she posts the wrong thing, give ourselves grace when we follow the wrong person, and to lean on the grace of God as we seek to lift others up as we bring them racing alongside us toward Heaven.

Who should I follow? The only answer is Jesus, the only One who is able to make our lives worthy of a race well run. With all of our eyes together set on the Savior, we're taking baby steps and giant leaps toward the Kingdom of God.

PRAYERS & PRAISES

CONVERSATION

1. What's your social media situation looking like these days? Mark what most fits you below, then explain why you chose that answer.

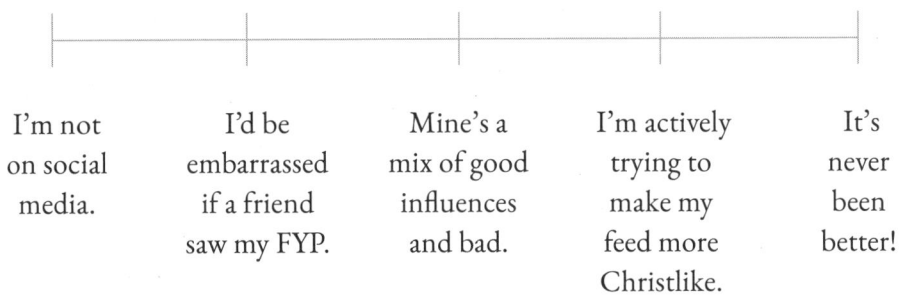

I'm not on social media.	I'd be embarrassed if a friend saw my FYP.	Mine's a mix of good influences and bad.	I'm actively trying to make my feed more Christlike.	It's never been better!

2. We are called to follow those who follow Jesus. Are you being intentionally discipled by an older Christian woman right now? Would you like to be? Why or why not? (Bonus! Brainstorm two or three older women of faith you could ask to disciple you.)

3. Christian community helps us grow in our faith. Are you plugged into a local church in this season? If yes, how can you dive even deeper into community at your church? If not, what do you think has been holding you back?

4. What's one way you can be a witness for Christ on your social media platforms this week?

09

HOW DO I READ THE BIBLE?

HOW DO I READ THE BIBLE?

PHILIPPIANS 4:1-9

Are you the girl who loves reading her Bible but wants some new ways to dive deeper? Are you the girl who's brand new to reading the Word and wants to learn some helpful tips and tricks? Are you the girl who hasn't cracked open the dusty Bible under her dorm room bed all semester? Wherever you're at in your Bible reading journey, this chapter is for you!

In this chapter, we're covering one of the simplest yet most powerful ways to grow in your faith: diving into the Word of God.

Read Philippians 4:1-9.

We're jumping into the second half of the Scripture you just read for our study today, the portion directly after Paul calls out some drama in the church. (See, first century Christians were just like us!) And, I'm guessing these are verses you've come across before.

+ FILL IN THE BLANKS BELOW.

"Do not be ______________ about anything, but in every situation, by prayer and petition, with thanksgiving, present your requests to God. And the ______________ of God, which transcends all understanding, will guard your hearts and your minds in Christ Jesus."
Philippians 4:6-7

+ FILL IN THE BLANKS BELOW.

"Finally, brothers and sisters, whatever is ______________ , whatever is noble, whatever is ______________ , whatever is pure, whatever is lovely, whatever is ______________ –if anything is excellent or praiseworthy–think about such things."
Philippians 4:8

Were you almost able to fill in those blanks from memory? Me, too! If Paul had a highlight reel of hall-of-fame verses, these would make the list. They're so good and so clear and so relevant that we hear them all the time. You'll see them on cool Christian graphic T's, written on cutesy coffee mugs, and—I kid you not—Philippians 4:6-7 is actually my Wifi password.

But can I be real with you? I think it's those verses I hear all the time that can begin to feel the least impactful. Yes, they're good and clear and relevant, but they're *so* good and clear and relevant that they become obscure, mystical, and frankly kind of boring when we become desensitized to their true weight.

NOTES:

Can you relate to this feeling? I wonder if it's a subtle trick of the enemy. He wants us to ignore the very real power of God's Word, so He twists God's Word to seem commonplace and not worth exploring any deeper.

All this leads us to the question we're asking this week . . . *How do I read the Bible?* If we believe that God's Word is perfect and powerful, how can we read it and interact with it in a way that supports that belief?

Now, I'm not going to pretend I have all the answers. There are lots and lots of ways to interact with Scripture and enough good advice about it to fill up thousands of books. Instead, what I want is to prompt your heart to go a little bit deeper. My hope is that, by the end of this chapter, you'll feel a little bit more confident in your Bible skills and a little bit more fired up to read it.

THINK IT THROUGH

+ If you're being honest, how do you currently feel about reading your Bible? (Find yourself on the scale below.)

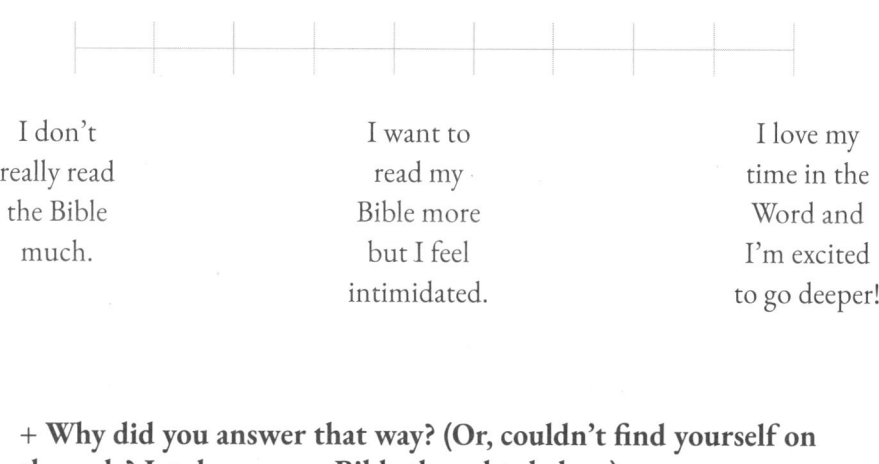

I don't really read the Bible much.	I want to read my Bible more but I feel intimidated.	I love my time in the Word and I'm excited to go deeper!

+ Why did you answer that way? (Or, couldn't find yourself on the scale? Jot down your Bible thoughts below.)

We're going to practice our Bible reading skills together on this portion of Philippians. Let's see if God can make these famous verses fresh again!

STOP & PRAY

GOD, THANK YOU FOR THE GIFT OF YOUR WORD. PLEASE OPEN MY EYES TO THE POWER YOUR SCRIPTURE HOLDS AND TEACH ME HOW TO LOVE MY BIBLE EVEN MORE.

Re-read Philippians 4:4-9.

01 READ THE BIBLE LIKE IT'S ABOUT GOD

You might have heard me say it before and you'll probably hear me say it again, but I believe one of the most dangerous ways to interact with Scripture is to assume it's all about you. That's like going to your best friend's birthday party and expecting everyone to give you presents; it just doesn't make sense! Scripture is God's party. It's a holy and beautiful representation of the heart of God. It's literally *God-breathed* (2 Timothy 3:16-17). And when we approach it with selfish intentions, we're missing the whole point.

Look back at what we just read in Philippians. If it's about me, I'm reading it to learn that I'm anxious (v6), that I don't understand (v7), and that I want peace (v 9). Starting with that rather obvious train of thought, I'd be led to assume I can fix myself by choosing not to be anxious, by being better at prayer, and by thinking about the right things.

But, have you ever tried not to be anxious? It's pretty tough to just decide to not be anxious anymore. Have you tried to tame your mind in your own power or pick up a new spiritual discipline off the cuff? It's hard; some might even say impossible! Reading the Bible that way will leave us burnt out, striving, and disenchanted with God's design for our lives. I mean, if that's how we want to approach Scripture we might as well just buy the newest self-help book and move on.

But, look back at Philippians 4:4-9 and look for God first, not yourself. Can you see the difference?

Suddenly, I read verse 4 and I learn that I have *a Lord worth rejoicing in.* I read verse 5 and I learn that *God is near.* I read verse 6 and I learn that *my God loves to hear my requests,* ever so patient with me as I tell him about my struggles. I read verse 7 and I realize that *God is overflowing with a peace He loves to share with me.* I read verse 9 and I see that *God's peace will be with me.*

Reading Scripture with a "God lens" sets our heart on Him and reorients everything in our lives back into right alignment. We were created to adore God, to gaze on His glory (Psalm 27:4). When we approach His Word by beginning there, in adoration of who He is, things start to fall into place much more naturally than if we were trying to help ourselves.

Now here's the crazy part. Yes, the Bible is all *about* God, but it also can be *for* you!

"All Scripture is God-breathed and is useful for teaching, rebuking, correcting and training in righteousness, so that the servant of God may be thoroughly equipped for every good work."
2 Timothy 3:16-17

As selfish as we can tend to be, our God is the opposite. He is the most self-giving person ever! His very Word, a Holy Spirit-filled representation of His heart and His glory, is given to us as a gift to teach us, correct us, train us, and equip us! We need to start with God, yes, but through that heart posture God starts a work on us. That ever-available and patient God of peace we read about in Philippians 4:4-9 empowers us to meditate on good things, rely on God's peace, and find an answer to our anxiety we could never have mustered up on our own.

Y'all, this is one of my favorite Bible reading tips ever! It's so simple yet so life changing. Every time you sit down to read Scripture, start by looking for God first. And just watch as His Word comes alive to you in a new way.

+ Let's practice! Flip to Psalm 27 in your Bible and read the whole chapter. What would a "me-centered" reading of the text be? How would a "God-focused" reading be different?

You know what question makes me sweat? When people ask me what commentaries I use when I study for these books. *Uhhh, what if they don't like that theologian? Do they know of a better one I'm missing? Why am I suddenly forgetting every commentary I've ever read?*

If you didn't know, there are some really cool tools for Bible study called "commentaries" written by theologians who go verse by verse through a specific Bible and make observations about the text. As the name suggests, they "comment" on the Scripture, giving context and helping you form an informed opinion about what you're reading.

KEEP GROWING

ARE YOU WANTING TO DIP YOUR TOE INTO THE WORLD OF BIBLICAL COMMENTARIES? ENDURING WORD IS A GREAT FREE RESOURCE ONLINE! SIMPLY TYPE "ENDURING WORD" AND THE CHAPTER YOU'RE STUDYING INTO THE GOOGLE SEARCH BAR AND IT WILL POP UP. OR, DOWNLOAD THE APP!

I guess you could even define this study as a commentary of sorts. I studied Philippians and now I'm using what I learned to help you study Philippians. But, as amazing as commentaries and Bible studies are as resources to go deeper in the Word, I think we can tend to jump straight to what other people tell us to think about a certain piece of Scripture before we sit and listen to what *God* wants us to receive from it. And, like we talked about last week, sometimes other people aren't necessarily the best to learn from if they aren't actively following the example of Christ.

So here's the safest way to read the Bible, the best way to start out before you start bringing outside sources into the mix: use the Bible to read the Bible.

02 USE THE BIBLE TO READ THE BIBLE

Did you know that the Bible cross references itself 63,779 times? Yeah, that's a *wild* number! It's just more evidence of the divine inspiration of Scripture. Only God could write a book that intricate and well-planned. Anywhere you're reading in Scripture, there's more than likely another point in Scripture that relates to what you're reading, takes the concept deeper, or explains something hard to understand.

So, when you're sitting with a certain passage and you want a fuller understanding of what God may be trying to tell you through it, a great first step is to flip around in your Bible and see what God's Word says about it, even before you see what theologians, Christian authors, or your mentors have to say. (Hint: your Bible might even have relevant verses listed at the bottom of the page!)

Let's try this method out on our famous verses from Philippians.

Philippians 4:6 says, "Do not be anxious about anything, but in every situation, by prayer and petition, with thanksgiving, present your requests to God." Does the idea of presenting your requests to God ring a bell? It makes me think of the words of Jesus in Matthew 7.

> *"Ask and it will be given to you; seek and you will find; knock and the door will be opened to you. For everyone who asks receives; the one who seeks finds; and to the one who knocks, the door will be opened."*
> *Matthew 7:7-8*

I read that verse and I see a greater picture of the God who welcomes my questions and cares about what I'm going through. Not only am I empowered to present my requests to Him like I'm knocking on His door, but I also learn that I will actually *receive* what I'm asking for. All of the sudden, one little verse I use as a Wifi password opens up and becomes so much deeper and wider—the usefulness and equipping of God's Word in action!

+ Try it out! Use the Bible to read deeper into Philippians 4:7. Can you find any other verses that might inform your reading of this verse? (Hint: Jesus's words in John 14:27 would be a great place to start.)

We've learned to read the Bible like it's about God and we've learned to use the Bible to go deeper into the Bible. The last little Scripture tip we have for this week is one Paul loves to remind his readers of.

+ FILL IN THE BLANKS FROM PHILIPPIANS 4:9.

"Whatever you have learned or received or heard from me, or seen in me— __________ __________ __________ __________ . And the God of peace will be with you."

What you learn from God's Word is just knowledge until you *put it into practice.*

03 Practice What You Read

Let's put ourselves in Paul's shoes for a minute here. Imagine you poured your whole heart into a long-winded letter to people you love and feel responsible for. In that letter, you reminded them of important things that were critical to their success and called them higher out of your deep care for them. Once that masterpiece of a letter was delivered by hand, they read it out loud for the whole church. Then, when the whole letter had been read, they clapped and just moved on with their lives, never thinking about it again.

Uh, if I were Paul I would be mad. He wasn't just spewing good advice for them to appreciate and ignore. He wanted them to take action to live out their lives in a Christ-honoring way! Clearly, he intended them to *put into practice* all he had taught.

The concept is the same for us as modern readers of the Bible as it was for the Philippians. Yes, God wants us to appreciate the beauty of Scripture. But, if our appreciation just stops at reading, it's not lining up with His design.

James says it like this in his Epistle:

> *"Do not merely listen to the word, and so deceive yourselves. Do what it says."*
> *James 1:22*

"Deceive" is a key word there. Remember how the devil loves to make Scripture just cute sayings instead of life changing truth? He does that because he wants us to merely hear the Word and stop short of actually taking action. We are *deceived* if we think wearing a Bible verse on a bracelet is enough to experience the true intended power of the Word. When we take action—or act in obedience to what we read in the Bible—we are allowing the Holy Spirit to work in and through us, leading to a Kingdom-shaking breakthrough that makes the world look a little more like Heaven every day; and, that makes you look a little more like Jesus.

There's a lot of ways we can "put into practice" what Paul says in just these few short verses we've been meditating on. Check it out!

★ REJOICE IN THE LORD. (VERSE 4)

★ PRACTICE GENTLENESS. (VERSE 5)

★ FIGHT ANXIETY WITH PRAYER. (VERSE 6)

★ CHOOSE GRATITUDE. (VERSE 6)

★ MEDITATE ON WHAT IS TRUE, NOBLE, RIGHT, PURE, LOVELY, EXCELLENT, AND PRAISEWORTHY. (VERSE 8)

NOTES:

As we seek to obey what we read in the Word, I want to frame this in the correct context for us. I know it can feel like a to-do list, or even a "requirement" to be a good Christian. But, honestly, that's a bummer way to think about it! *Guys, "doing" Scripture makes your Bible time so much more fun!* The call to put what we read into practice isn't a beatdown, it's an invitation to allow your faith to spark to life in so many areas of your life, not just in your morning quiet time!

And, if you want to grow in your faith, you can't go wrong with simple obedience.

Here's a fun way to get started with practicing what we read in the Word: *memorize it.* When you find yourself in moments where you're choosing between doing what God's Word says and what your flesh wants you to do, the best way to fight back is by knowing the Scripture. Just like Jesus did when He was in the wilderness (Matthew 4), fight back against temptation with the Word of God.

+ Choose one verse from our reading this week (Philippians 4:1-9) to memorize. Copy it down below. (*Bonus!* Find an accountability partner to make sure you actually follow through.)

Wow! That felt a little bit like drinking from a fire hose, but I hope you feel a little bit more equipped and a lot more excited to dive into God's Word than you did before reading this chapter. As we seek to stand firm in our faith (Philippians 4:1), there's nothing better than learning to love God's Word.

> *"Your word is a lamp for my feet, a light on my path."*
> *Psalm 119:105*

+ **Here's a little cheat sheet for Bible reading based on what we learned this week! Write this on a sticky note and put it in your Bible to keep handy.**

★ READ WITH A GOD-FOCUS.
★ CROSS REFERENCE OTHER BIBLE VERSES.
★ USE A BIBLICAL COMMENTARY.
★ PUT WHAT YOU READ INTO PRACTICE.
★ MEMORIZE SCRIPTURE.

OTHER TIPS AND TRICKS:

WHERE DO I START? →
The Gospel of John is a great place to start!

WHAT IF I'M NOT GOOD AT IT? →
Start small and don't compare yourself to others!

WHAT TRANSLATION SHOULD I USE? →
We use the NIV translation at Delight!

WHERE CAN I FIND A BIBLE READING PLAN? →
We love using the plans on the Bible App!

HOW DO I STAY CONSISTENT? →
Do it in community!
(i.e. find an accountability partner.)

PRAYERS & PRAISES

CONVERSATION

1. In this chapter we learned three ways to go deeper in Scripture (reading the Bible like it's about God, using the Bible to read the Bible, and practicing what we read). Which of these are you most confident in? Which are you most excited to grow in?

2. What stands out to you from Philippians 4:1-9? What lessons can you take away from them?

3. What is your current Bible reading routine? How would you like it to grow or change?

4. Consider . . . What book of the Bible would you like to study after we finish reading Philippians? Why did you choose that one? Can you think of any Bible plans, resources, or sermons that might help you in your study?

10

WHAT NOW?

What Now?

PHILIPPIANS 4:10-23

When I was in college, my friend had this bright idea for us to get in shape. We were going to fully embrace our fit girl era—stopping by the campus rec center every day, eating salads for lunch, and spending a large percentage of our barista paychecks on cute workout clothes.

And let me tell you—we went *hard*. For a solid week and a half we hit up the gym every day, did our homework on the treadmills, and checked in on each other's grocery hauls to make sure everything was organic. I was flying high, exhausted from the exercise but fired up by my new lease on life.

Then, right around the two-week mark, I noticed in the mirror that I was looking a little more toned. I seemed healthier, more awake, and generally a leveled-up version of me. So, naturally, *I quit immediately.*

In my mind, I'd done what I set out to do. I got healthy! I did the hard work and reaped the rewards. Why would I keep putting myself through that grueling regime if the results were there? (If you can't tell, self discipline isn't my strong suit.) So, I stopped all the work and patted myself on the back for getting my life together.

As you can probably assume, my new healthy glow quickly faded. My energy dropped, my gym membership expired, and my backpack got a little bit harder to carry around campus. But my friend wasn't ready to give up as easily. She kept it up, stayed disciplined, and her healthy glow stayed around. She kept getting fitter and fitter, reaping the reward of her consistency and persistence.

Now, this is not meant to be exercise propaganda. If you're looking for workout tips, I'm certainly not the girl to ask. But, I do think what I experienced in my fit-girl era is what a lot of us go through as we seek to grow in our faith.

We go to Bible study every single week for the whole semester, amped about the accountability. But, when the season ends, we fall off the wagon without the group's support to back us up.

We find the perfect Bible study to level up in that specific area of our faith we feel weak in, and we actually see growth for a few weeks. Then, once the study is completed and takes up residence on our dusty bookshelf, our habits go back to the way they've always been.

We do a 30-day prayer challenge and see so much depth in our intimacy with the Lord as we finally commit to giving Him more of our attention. But, on day 31, we snap back to being just a pray-before-meals kind of gal.

We're at the end of our 10-week study of the book of Philippians. And, while I hope you've experienced wild spiritual growth along the way, my hope is that you continue to grow long past the end of this Bible study. God's not interested in "get fit quick" schemes that fizzle out just as fast. He's in it for the long haul, ready to transform you bit by bit as you walk with Him throughout your life. He's willing to put in the years of building that will take you from where you are now to the wise old grandma we'd all like to be.

So, *what now?* How do we continue to grow in the days, years, and decades to come? How do we stay consistent with the things we learned throughout this study? How do we keep growing and growing and growing? I believe we can find the answer to that question and more in the final portion of Philippians we have left to explore. In what Paul wrote as his final reminders to the people of Philippi, we can find some final reminders for ourselves as well.

This doesn't have to be a spiritual high that fades. You can grow with God every day for the rest of your life.

Read Philippians 4:10-23.

STOP & PRAY

GOD, THANK YOU FOR ALL THE WAYS YOU HAVE SPOKEN TO ME AND POURED INTO ME THROUGHOUT THIS STUDY. I ASK THAT YOU WOULD SEAL IT ALL IN MY HEART AND ALLOW ME TO CONTINUE TO GROW AS I STEP INTO A NEW SEASON.

This last chunk of Philippians is a great opportunity to explore context. And, honestly, you don't have to dig too hard to figure out what Paul's talking about in his closing remarks.

+ Based on your reading of Philippians 4:10-23, what is Paul thanking the Philippians for?

+ Who delivered this financial gift to Paul?

+ Was this the first time the Philippian church sent a financial gift to Paul? (Circle yes or no.)

YES NO

If you remember back in Philippians chapter 2, Paul wrote about the messenger Epaphroditus overcoming an illness by God's power. Epaphroditus, a member of the church of Philippi, had been sent to visit Paul in his Roman imprisonment to deliver some money the church was donating to help take care of him. This is a huge thing for a couple of reasons: 1) That was an 800-mile journey before bicycles were invented and 2) Paul's imprisonment in Rome didn't come with a meal voucher; all of his basic needs had to be provided for by the generosity of his friends. So, it makes sense that Paul reserved a lot of real estate in his letter to thank them for their generosity in sending Epaphroditus and the money.

But, in typical Paul fashion, he didn't just stick with a simple "thank you." Instead, Paul uses it as a teaching moment on the way God cares for us and the lessons God had taught him in his life. It's sort of like a bonus lesson thrown in at the end, as if Paul couldn't end the letter without including these few important truths. And they're important truths that can definitely light the way in our "what now?" search.

Let's start in verse 11 where Paul mentions those life lessons.

+ FILL IN THE BLANKS FROM PHILIPPIANS 4:11.

"I am not saying this because I am in need, for I have ____________ to be ____________ whatever the ________________."

Here's the bottom line: As you continue on in your journey and step into the next season of life, there will be "circumstances" that hit you. And the fact of the matter is that those circumstances can either stall your growth or expedite it. Paul, as it seems, has learned the "secret" to allowing those circumstances to teach him.

> *"I know what it is to be in need, and I know what it is to have plenty. I have learned the secret of being content in any and every situation, whether well fed or hungry, whether living in plenty or in want."*
> *Philippians 4:12*

01 LET LIFE TEACH YOU LESSONS.

I'll be real with you. If I were in prison and relying solely on the generosity of others for my basic needs, I wouldn't tell my gracious benefactors that I'd be fine without them. On the contrary! I'd be hyping them up so much, all but begging them to keep sending me coffee and prosciutto.

But somehow Paul felt differently. Sure, he was grateful for the help, but he knew how to be OK whether help came or it didn't. And how did he learn that? Well, we can find the answer in his letters to the Corinthians.

+ Find 2 Corinthians 11:23-28. List Paul's trials and sufferings below.

Because of what he had been through (which was a *lot*), Paul knew that he would survive whatever came next. The result of his trials was a godly kind of contentment, one that can't really be found without some kind of ordeal. If you're honest, have your own trials and ordeals built contentment in you? Or, did they foster something else, something more along the lines of fear, bitterness, apathy, or disenchantment?

If you want to grow in your faith, welcoming trials (or, weathering the storms of life in a God-honoring way) is not only necessary, but it's pretty much a requirement. Because trials are going to come. And, if every one brings you further away from Jesus instead of closer to His heart, you will find yourself 20 years down the road wondering how you got so far from the strong faith you had at the start.

Paul's not the only biblical author who addresses learning from life. Here's what James has to say about it:

"Consider it pure joy, my brothers and sisters, whenever you face trials of many kinds, because you know that the testing of your faith produces perseverance. Let perseverance finish its work so that you may be mature and complete, not lacking anything."
James 1:2-4

+ Look back at the verse above and circle "let."

We are called to *let* or *allow* the storms and trials of life to make us more Christlike. It's an intentionality to suffering we don't often consider. What if that season of your life, however hard it may be, doesn't have to be wasted? I believe it's possible to come out the other side stronger and more like Jesus than you were before. Miraculously, God can even shift your perspective. You can *consider it pure joy* that you encountered that trial, as backwards as that seems.

I'm not glad my mother-in-law died, but I'm glad to be able to encourage my friends who are grieving.

I'm not glad about the years of infertility, but I'm glad for the intentionality in motherhood the years of waiting taught me.

I'm not glad for the years of sickness I underwent in college, but I'm glad for the way it redirected my life for the better.

NOTES:

+ What about you? Think about a trial in your past. How might God have used it to mature you?

So, *what now?* Well, the first step is to have that fresh perspective on your next trial and to allow it to teach you vital lessons. And, one of those lessons—one that Paul certainly learned—is dependency on Christ.

02 DEPEND ON GOD'S STRENGTH

> *"I can do all this through him who gives me strength."*
> *Philippians 4:13*

I believe a lot of us take this verse out of its original context and twist it for our own gain, whether intentionally or not. We use this verse to reinforce a "triumphalist" or "super-Christian" mentality.[1] We assume it means that we can literally do anything because we have God on our team. He's a genie in a bottle ready to grant all of our wishes. But, that's not what Paul's saying here and that's also not how God rolls.

First of all, Paul's still talking about contentment here. He's saying that God gives him the strength to stay OK whether rich or poor. But, even if we expand this biblical principle in light of the entire Bible, we find another important caveat.

+ Find John 15:5 and copy it down in the space below.

Jesus says that apart from Him, we can do *nothing*. So Philippians 4:13 doesn't mean that we can face anything in life and expect to win because we're a Christian. You can't assume God will bless a decision you know is against His will. You can't expect God to help you out in a sinful endeavor. You can't blindly jump into a dangerous situation because you believe you're invincible. *That ain't it, sis!* If you're out of His will and His design, nothing will succeed the way you're hoping it will.

KEEP GROWING

ARE YOU STRUGGLING TO DISCERN WHAT IS IN THE WILL OF GOD AND WHAT ISN'T? TRY TESTING IT AGAINST SCRIPTURE! IF THE BIBLE DISAGREES WITH YOU, YOU'RE IN THE DANGER ZONE!

Instead, we should read this verse as an invitation to deepen our *dependency* on Christ. It's His strength that gives us the power to follow His call. When we learn how to rely on that strength and ditch our attempts at being independent, a whole new world of growth and spiritual maturity opens up to us.

Let's make this super practical. As you go out into the world and step into whatever season God has in store for you next, practice asking God for His strength. Did He ask you to apply for a job you feel is way out of your league? Pray for His strength as you walk into the job interview. Did He ask you to break up with that toxic boyfriend? Pray for His strength as you begin that hard conversation.

Is He asking you to grow? Ask for His strength to do it. Because it's through His strength that all things are possible.

+ Consider . . . What area of your life right now do you need more of God's strength for?

Ummm, I'm starting to freak out a little bit here . . . How are we already on the last point of the last chapter of our *Room To Grow* study? This flew by way too fast! I think we need to stop and reflect before we wrap things up.

+ Flip back through the rest of the study. Which chapter stood out to you the most? What did you learn from it?

As I read through these parting words from Paul, one last verse pricks my heart. It's a verse I want us to meditate on as we're sent out into what God has in store for us next.

"And my God will meet all your needs according to the riches of his glory in Christ Jesus."
Philippians 4:19

How was Paul able to so confidently declare that God would meet all of their needs? Because he had his *hope* firmly planted in the glory of Christ Jesus.

03 He Will Supply Your Needs

We're going to need to jump somewhere else in the Bible to really nail down this concept. (Shoutout to last week! Use the Bible to read the Bible!) Charles Spurgeon, one of the most famous theologians ever, compared Paul's expectant hope in the riches of Jesus's glory to a story all the way back in 2 Kings.[2] Let's check it out.

Read 2 Kings 4:1-7.

+ In your own words, summarize what happened in the Scripture you just read.

This is one of those really cool stories in the Bible that you could meditate on for years and still get something new out of it! Essentially, God used his prophet Elisha to help a poor widow in need. It was a provision miracle where, as she poured oil into empty jars she'd collected, it just kept coming and coming. By the end, she had enough of the miraculous oil to sell it and pay off her debts.

NOTES:

This adds so much depth to what we read in Philippians 4! God is so good that He fills our needs over and above what we could even imagine. Even a hopeless situation can be turned into something miraculous. As the woman kept pouring, God's glorious riches kept providing.

But, did you notice that when she ran out of jars, the oil ran out as well?

"When all the jars were full, she said to her son, 'Bring me another one.' But he replied, 'There is not a jar left.' Then the oil stopped flowing."
2 Kings 4:6

It makes me wonder . . . If she had collected more jars, would God have provided even more oil? Think of those empty jars as our hope—our expectancy that God will *meet all of [our] needs according to the riches of his glory in Christ Jesus* (v 19). God, in His riches, is happy to fill and fulfill every "jar" of hope. But if we only offer Him one little jar, is there more of His provision we could be missing out on because we didn't dare to dream that He could provide in that way?

NOTES:

Have you ever found yourself praying a smaller prayer because it feels more realistic? Instead of, *God please miraculously heal my friend of her cancer,* we pray, *God please make her comfortable.* Instead of, *God please give me my dream job,* we pray, *God please let this interview not go as badly as the last.* Instead of, *God please bring me my future husband*, we pray, *God help me go on one more date.*

Of course, there's something to be said for humility and submission to God's will and how that affects the way we pray, but I think that if we truly believe in the riches of glory we have access to in Christ Jesus, we would be hoping bigger, praying bigger, and believing bigger.

THINK IT THROUGH

+ In the jars below, fill in some of the things you're hoping for in this next season.

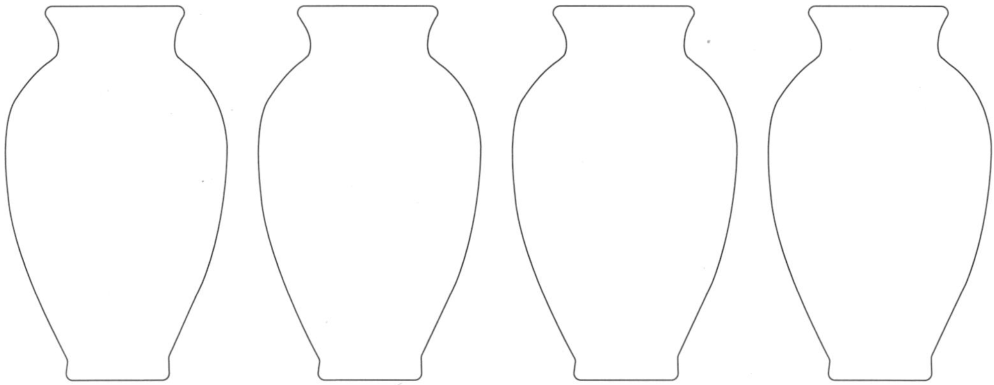

+ How might God be asking you to grow your hope in these areas?

When we walk with Jesus, we're growing bit by bit. He's letting us take baby steps as our "love abound[s] more and more in knowledge and depth of insight" (Philippians 2:9). It's a lifelong process of questions and answers, tears and laughs, and a whole lot of Christian community. My hope for you as you step into the next phase of your Christian walk—the next stage of spiritual maturity God has in store for you—is that God would open up your heart to His leading. As you allow Him to teach you through the ups and downs of life, as you rely on His strength, and as you keep the hope, I believe there is something beautiful waiting for you right around the corner.

I'm so glad God gives us room to grow. Because I'm not there yet, but I think I'm getting a little bit closer every day.

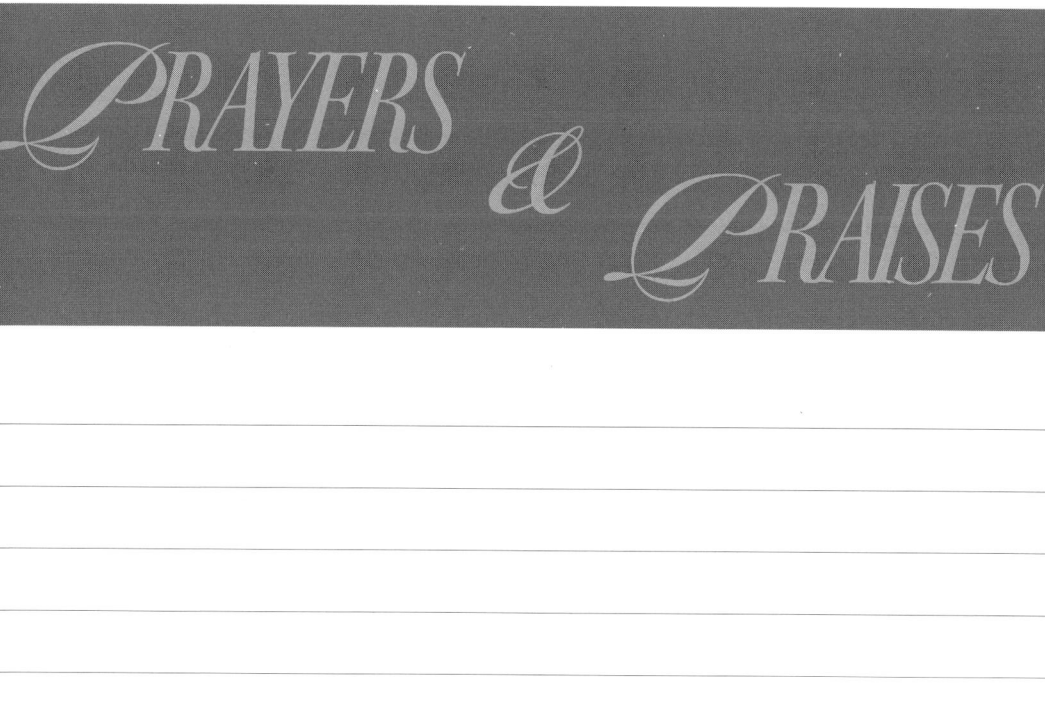

PRAYERS & PRAISES

CONVERSATION

1. Paul allowed the Lord to teach him lessons through the trials in his life. What lessons have your own trials taught you? How does that change your perspective on future trials you might encounter?

2. Philippians 4:13 is a famous Bible verse. How does reading it in context change your understanding of its meaning?

3. Look back at the jars of hope you filled in on page 200. Do you pray big prayers in these areas? Why or why not?

4. Take a moment and flip through the chapters of our study. How has your faith grown or matured throughout this exploration of Philippians?

NOTES

Chapter 1

1. N.T. Wright, Paul for Everyone: The Prison Letters: Ephesians, Philippians, Colossians, and Philemon (London, England: Westminster John Knox Press, 2002), 84

2. David Guzik, Philippians and Colossians: Verse by Verse Commentary (Goleta, CA: Enduring Word, 2019), 7

3. N.T. Wright, Paul for Everyone: The Prison Letters: Ephesians, Philippians, Colossians, and Philemon (London, England: Westminster John Knox Press, 2002), 86

4. D.A. Carson, Basics for Believers: An Exposition of Philippians (Grand Rapids, MI: Baker Publishing Group, 1996), 20

Chapter 3

1. David Guzik, Philippians and Colossians: Verse by Verse Commentary (Goleta, CA: Enduring Word, 2019), 19

2. David Guzik, Philippians and Colossians: Verse by Verse Commentary (Goleta, CA: Enduring Word, 2019)

3. Francis Foulkes, "Philippians," in New Bible Commentary: 21st Century Edition, ed. D. A. Carson et al., 4th ed. (Leicester, England; Downers Grove, IL: Inter-Varsity Press, 1994), 1252.

Chapter 5

1. Robert P. Lightner, "Philippians," in The Bible Knowledge Commentary: An Exposition of the Scriptures, ed. J. F. Walvoord and R. B. Zuck, vol. 2 (Wheaton, IL: Victor Books, 1985), 656.

Chapter 6

1. Paul Barnett, Philippians & Philemon: Joy in the Lord, ed. Paul Barnett, Reading the Bible Today Series (Sydney, South NSW: Aquila Press, 2016), 84.

2. Richard R. Melick Jr., "Philippians," in CSB Study Bible: Notes, ed. Edwin A. Blum and Trevin Wax (Nashville, TN: Holman Bible Publishers, 2017), 1887.

3. David Guzik, Philippians and Colossians: Verse by Verse Commentary (Goleta, CA: Enduring Word, 2019), 45

Chapter 10

1. David Guzik, Philippians and Colossians: Verse by Verse Commentary (Goleta, CA: Enduring Word, 2019), 62

2. David Guzik, Philippians and Colossians: Verse by Verse Commentary (Goleta, CA: Enduring Word, 2019), 64

CONTRIBUTORS

Editing Team:

Theological Editing by Aubrey Meredith

Editing by Madison Perry

Design:

Faith Hyman

Special thanks to . . .

Abby Elias

Alexa Ramirez

Anna Claire Lunger

Briley Bowers

Ella McFadyen

Ella McKinney

Emmy Mader

Natalie Krekeler

Rona Okojie

Tori Vatcher

ABOUT THE AUTHOR

Hey! I'm Maggie!

I am working my *dream job* as Creative Director here at Delight Ministries. I like to think of myself as Delight's translator. My job is to take God's powerful, perfect, and active Word and present it to college women in a way that helps them see how relevant it is for their own lives . . . *AND I LOVE IT!*

On the weekends, catch me serving in my church's kids ministry with my husband and hanging out with our ADORABLE baby, Sunny. I love to read, I'm a die-hard Swiftie, and I'll never say no to a *Twilight* marathon.

DELIGHT WORSHIP

It all started with a question . . . *What if we could write worship music for college women?*

SO WE DID! Delight Worship is intentional music created to connect college women to the heart of Jesus.

Listen today!

START A DELIGHT

Help us spread the word about Delight!

There are thousands of college women all across the country who need Christ-centered community but have no idea Delight exists! We need women like you to help spread the word.

If this community has impacted your life in any way, don't you want to help other women experience it, too?

If you know a friend who loves Jesus and would make an amazing Delight leader, tell her about Delight! With just a few texts you could indirectly reach hundreds of college women on another campus!

How cool is that!?

https://www.delightministries.com/start-a-chapter

Point your friends to our website where they can sign up to bring Delight to their campuses! Once they sign up, they will hear from us and will be equipped to get this community started at their university.

So . . . send a couple texts, call a couple friends, maybe post about it on your socials, and let's reach a million more college women together!

YEARBOOK PAGE

Fill these pages with sweet notes from your Delight community!

For more information, resources,
or encouragement head to . . .

www.delightministries.com